INTERNET OF THINGS
AND
EDGE COMPUTING
Simply In Depth

IoT using Arduino, Raspberry PI and
Windows 10 IoT Core

A J I T   S I N G H

IoT, IPv6, 6LoWPAN, EDGE FRAMEWORK
DESIGN, EDGE ARCHITECTURE, MOBILE EDGE
COMPUTING, EDGE COMPUTING IN IOT & IIOT,

Internet of Things and Edge Computing
Simply In Depth

Ajit Singh
e: ajit_singh24@yahoo.com

Table of Contents

About the Book

Edge computing for the Internet of Things (IoT) allows IoT deployments to be enhanced through data processing closer to the end device. This results in lower latency and improved efficiencies in data transport.

IoT edge computing is significantly different from non-IoT edge computing, with distinct demands and considerations. IoT devices typically have limited data processing and storage capabilities, so substantial data processing needs to occur off the device, with the edge offering an environment to undertake this processing and manage large volumes of IoT devices and data. This, in turn, can reduce device cost, as many functions can be off-loaded to the edge. The location of the edge itself has various possibilities and will differ according to the use case. For example, the edge for IoT could reside at an operator"s local or regional data centre, at a base station or at a dedicated server on the customer"s premises.

IoT market analysts expect the edge to play a significant role in supporting IoT implementations going forward, as it creates efficiencies and scale in networks that makes IoT deployments more self-sustaining. IDC (International Data Corporation) estimates that that by 2022, IT spending on edge infrastructure will reach up to 18 percent of the total spend on IoT infrastructure. Mobile operators have the demonstrable capability to manage infrastructure, data and applications for IoT services, and are well placed to continue this with edge for IoT.

This book facilitates and features the IoT technologies with respect to Edge Computing. I tried to cover from evolution, architecture, implementation and standard role of IoT along with the Edge Computing. The things are covered along with in-depth industry's real-life and practical use cases from industry.

The Internet of Things can be characterized as joining the physical object, the computer embedded into it, and communication and code on the Internet itself. I focused on these three elements in both the prototyping and the manufacturing sections. I began by looking at some examples of the Internet of Things in action.

In this book, I look at the kinds of computer chips that can be embedded in objects ("microcontrollers" such as the Arduino) and take you through each step of the process from prototyping a Thing to manufacturing and selling it. I explored the platforms you can use to develop the hardware and software. Throughout the book, i discussed many REAL LIFE projects, I have tried to cover introduction, implementation of IoT using Arduino and RASPBERRY PI along with suitable Case Studies.

This book is aimed to the curriculum of the IoT and Edge Computing course at prominent global Universities / Institutions of the World.

Acknowledgements

I would like to thank all the people who have helped me put together this book. Most of all, I would like to thank you, the reader, for trusting me to help you learn about Edge Computing.

The acknowledgements section was one I never normally paid a lot of attention to, as it was the author thanking a load of people I didn't know. Having written a book, and realized how much help and support are given to the authors, I have a newfound appreciation for this section

Chapter 1.
The Internet of Things (IoT)

Building upon a complex network connecting billions of devices and humans into a multi-technology, multi-protocol and multi-platform infrastructure, the Internet-of-Things (IoT) main vision is to create an intelligent world where the physical, the digital and the virtual are converging to create smart environments that provide more intelligence to the energy, health, transport, cities, industry, buildings and many other areas of our daily life.

A number of significant technology changes have come together to enable the rise of IoT. The prices of IoT hardware are dropping, putting sensors, processing power, network bandwidth, and cloud storage within reach of more users and making a wider range of IoT applications practical.

We define "the Internet of Things" as sensors and actuators connected by networks to computing systems. These systems can monitor or manage the health and actions of connected objects and machines. Connected sensors can also monitor the natural world, people, and animals.

The expectation is that of interconnecting millions of islands of smart networks enabling access to the information not only "anytime" and "anywhere" but also using "anything" and "anyone" ideally through any "path", "network" and "any service". This will be achieved by having the objects that we manipulate daily to be outfitted with sensing, identification and positioning devices and endowed with an IP address to become smart objects, capable of communicating with not only other smart objects but also with humans with the expectation of reaching areas that we could never reach without the advances made in the sensing, identification and positioning technologies.

We also observe the emergence of an Internet of Things ecosystem, another enabler of adoption. This includes vendors that specialize in IoT hardware and software, systems integrators, and a growing community of commercial and consumer IoT users.7 The actions of policy makers can advance or retard the evolution of the Internet of Things from this point. As we will discuss in Chapter 4, the potential economic impact that we estimate for IoT applications in 2025 depends on measures to make IoT data secure, protect personal privacy and intellectual property, and encourage interoperability among IoT devices and systems. Particularly in developing economies, low-cost data infrastructure is needed. Government agencies, working with technology providers, businesses, and consumers, can also participate in many of these efforts.

Finally, applying IoT technologies to human activities is already showing potential for massive change in people's lives. From giving people with chronic diseases new tools to manage their conditions to increasing fitness to avoid disease, the Internet of Things is beginning to demonstrate its potential to improve human health. Across the uses of IoT technology that we document in this report, people are the major beneficiaries—reducing their commuting times, offloading domestic chores to machines, saving money on energy, getting greater value from retail offers and in consumer products designed with IoT data, and enjoying life in safer homes and cities.

While being globally discoverable and queried, these smart objects can similarly discover and interact with external entities by querying humans, computers and other smart objects. The smart objects can also obtain intelligence by making or enabling context related decisions taking advantage of the available communication channels to provide information about themselves while also accessing information that has been aggregated by other smart objects.

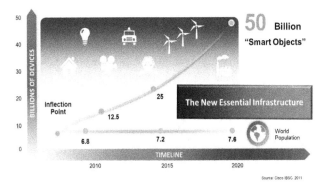

Figure 1. Internet-connected devices and the future evolution (Source: Cisco, 2011)

As revealed by Figure 1, the IoT is the new essential infrastructure which is predicted to connect 50 billion of smart objects in 2020 when the world population will reach 7.6 billion.

As suggested by the ITU, such essential infrastructure will be built around a multi-layered architecture where the smart objects will be used to deliver different services through the four main layers depicted by Figure 2: a device layer, a network layer, a support layer and the application layer.

In the device layer lie devices (sensors, actuators, RFID devices) and gateways used to collect the sensor readings for further processing while the network layer provides the necessary transport and networking capabilities for routing the IoT data to processing places. The support layer is a middleware layer that serves to hide the complexity of the lower layers to the application layer and provide specific and generic services such as storage in different forms (database management systems and/or cloud computing systems) and many other services such as translation.

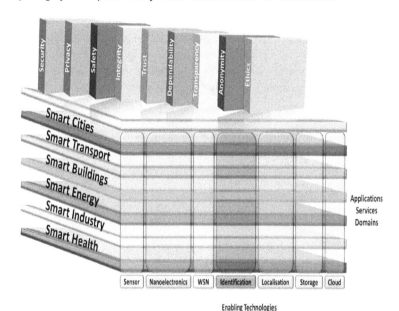

Figure 2. IoT Layered Architecture (Source: ITU-T)

The IoT can be perceived as an infrastructure driving a number of applications services which are enabled by a number of technologies. Its application services expand across many domains such as smart cities, smart transport, smart buildings, smart energy, smart industry and smart health while it is enabled by different technologies such as sensing, nanoeletronics, wireless sensor network (WSN), radio frequency identification (RFID), localization, storage and cloud. The IoT systems and

11

applications are designed to provide security, privacy, safety, integrity, trust, dependability, transparency, anonymity and are bound by ethics constraints.

Experts say we are heading towards what can be called a "ubiquitous network society", one in which networks and networked devices are omnipresent. RFID and wireless sensors promise a world of networked and interconnected devices that provide relevant content and information whatever the location of the user. Everything from tires to toothbrushes will be in communications range, heralding the dawn of a new era, one in which today's Internet (of data and people) gives way to tomorrow's Internet of Things.

At the dawn of the Internet revolution, users were amazed at the possibility of contacting people and information across the world and across time zones. The next step in this technological revolution (connecting people any-time, anywhere) is to connect inanimate objects to a communication network. This vision underlying the Internet of things will allow the information to be accessed not only "anytime" and "anywhere" but also by "anything".

This will be facilitated by using WSNs and RFID tags to extend the communication and monitoring potential of the network of networks, as well as the introduction of computing power in everyday items such as razors, shoes and packaging.

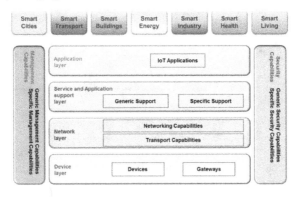

Figure 3 : IoT Application Stack

WSNs are an early form of ubiquitous information and communication networks. They are one of building blocks of the Internet of things.

Wireless Sensor Networks

A Wireless Sensor Network (WSN) is a self-configuring network of small sensor nodes (so-called motes) communicating among them using radio signals, and deployed in quantity to sense the physical world. Sensor nodes are essentially small computers with extremely basic functionality. They consist of a processing unit with limited computational power and limited memory, a radio communication device, a power source and one or more sensors.

Motes come in different sizes and shapes, depending on their foreseen use. They can be very small, if they are to be deployed in big numbers and need to have little visual impact. They can have a rechargeable battery power source if they are to be used in a lab. The integration of these tiny, ubiquitous electronic devices in the most diverse scenarios ensures a wide range of applications. Some of the application areas are environmental monitoring, agriculture, health and security.

In a typical application, a WSN is scattered in a region where it is meant to collect data through its sensor nodes. These networks provide a bridge between the physical world and the virtual world. They promise unprecedented abilities to observe and understand large scale, real-world phenomena at a fine spatio-temporal resolution. This is so because one deploys sensor nodes in large numbers directly in the field, where the experiments take place. All motes are composed of five main elements as shown below:

1. Processor: the task of this unit is to process locally sensed information and information sensed by other devices. At present the processors are limited in terms of computational power, but given Moore's law, future devices will come in smaller sizes, will be more powerful and consume less energy. The processor can run in different modes: sleep is used most of the time to save power, idle is used when data can arrive from other motes, and active is used when data is sensed or sent to / received from other motes.

2. Power source: motes are meant to be deployed in various environments, including remote and hostile regions so they must use little power. Sensor nodes typically have little energy storage, so networking protocols must emphasize power conservation. They also must have built-in

13

mechanisms that allow the end user the option of prolonging network lifetime at the cost of lower throughput. Sensor nodes may be equipped with effective power scavenging methods, such as solar cells, so they may be left unattended for months, or years. Common sources of power are rechargeable batteries, solar panels and capacitors.

3. Memory: it is used to store both programs (instructions executed by the processor) and data (raw and processed sensor measurements).

4. Radio: WSN devices include a low-rate, short-range wireless radio. Typical rates are 10-100 kbps, and range is less than 100 meters. Radio communication is often the most power-intensive task, so it is a must to incorporate energy-efficient techniques such as wake-up modes. Sophisticated algorithms and protocols are employed to address the issues of lifetime maximization, robustness and fault tolerance.

5. Sensors: sensor networks may consist of many different types of sensors capable of monitoring a wide variety of ambient conditions. Table 1 classifies the three main categories of sensors based on field-readiness and scalability. While scalability reveals if the sensors are small and inexpensive enough to scale up to many distributed systems, the field-readiness describes the sensor's engineering efficiency with relation to field deployment. In terms of the engineering efficiency, Table 1 reveals high field-readiness for most physical sensors and for a few chemical sensors since most chemical sensors lie in the medium and low levels, while biological sensors have low field-readiness.

Sensor Category	Parameter	Field-Readiness	Scalability
Physical	Temperature	High	High
	Moisture Content	High	High
	Flow rate, Flow velocity	High	Med-High
	Pressure	High	High
	Light Transmission (Turb)	High	High
Chemical	Dissolved Oxygen	High	High
	Electrical Conductivity	High	High
	pH	High	High
	Oxydation Reduction Potential	Medium	High
	Major Ionic Species (Cl-, Na+)	Low-Medium	High
	Nutrientsa (Nitrate, Ammonium)	Low-Medium	Low-High
	Heavy metals	Low	Low
	Small Organic Compounds	Low	Low
	Large Organic Compounds	Low	Low
Biological	Microorganisms	Low	Low
	Biologically active contaminants	Low	Low

Common applications include the sensing of temperature, humidity, light, pressure, noise levels, acceleration, soil moisture, etc. Due to bandwidth and power constraints, devices primarily support low-data-units with limited computational power and limited rate of sensing.

Some applications require multi-mode sensing, so each device may have several sensors on board. Following is a short description of the technical characteristics of WSNs that make this technology attractive.

1. **Wireless Networking**: motes communicate with each other via radio in order to exchange and process data collected by their sensing unit. In some cases, they can use other nodes as relays, in which case the network is said to be multi-hop. If nodes communicate only directly with each other or with the gateway, the network is said to be single-hop. Wireless connectivity allows to retrieve data in real-time from locations that are difficult to access. It also makes the monitoring system less intrusive in places where wires would disturb the normal operation of the environment to monitor. It reduces the costs of installation: it has been estimated that wireless technology could eliminate up to 80 % of this cost.

2. **Self-organization**: motes organize themselves into an ad-hoc network, which means they do not need any pre-existing infrastructure. In WSNs, each mote is programmed to run a discovery of its neighborhood, to recognize which are the nodes that it can hear and talk to over its radio. The capacity of organizing spontaneously in a network makes them easy to deploy, expand and maintain, as well as resilient to the failure of individual points.

3. **Low-power**: WSNs can be installed in remote locations where power sources are not available. They must therefore rely on power given by batteries or obtained by energy harvesting techniques such as solar panels. In order to run for several months of years, motes must use low-power radios and processors and implement power efficient schemes. The processor must go to sleep mode as long as possible, and the Medium-Access layer must be designed accordingly. Thanks to these techniques, WSNs allow for long-lasting deployments in remote locations.

Applications of Wireless Sensor Networks

The integration of these tiny, ubiquitous electronic devices in the most diverse scenarios ensures a wide range of applications. Some of the most common application areas are environmental monitoring, agriculture, health and security. In a typical application, a WSN include:

1. Tracking the movement of animals. A large sensor network has been deployed to study the effect of micro climate factors in habitat selection of sea birds on Great Duck Island in Maine, USA. Researchers placed their sensors in burrows and used heat to detect the presence of nesting birds, providing invaluable data to biological researchers. The deployment was heterogeneous in that it employed burrow nodes and weather nodes.
2. Forest fire detection. Since sensor nodes can be strategically deployed in a forest, sensor nodes can relay the exact origin of the fire to the end users before the fire is spread uncontrollable. Researchers from the University of California, Berkeley, demonstrated the feasibility of sensor network technology in a fire environment with their FireBug application.

3. Flood detection. An example is the ALERT system deployed in the US. It uses sensors that detect rainfall, water level and weather conditions. These sensors supply information to a centralized database system.

4. Geophysical research. A group of researchers from Harvard deployed a sensor network on an active volcano in South America to monitor seismic activity and similar conditions related to volcanic eruptions.

5. Agricultural applications of WSN include precision agriculture and monitoring conditions that affect crops and livestock. Many of the problems in managing farms to maximize production while achieving environmental goals can only be solved with appropriate data. WSN can also be used in retail control, particularly in goods that require being maintained under controlled conditions (temperature, humidity, light intensity, etc) [SusAgri].

6. An application of WSN in security is predictive maintenance. BP's Loch Rannoch project developed a commercial system to be used in refineries. This system monitors critical rotating machinery to evaluate operation conditions and report when wear and tear is detected. Thus one can understand how a machine is wearing and perform predictive maintenance. Sensor networks can be used to detect chemical agents in the air and water. They can also help to identify the type, concentration and location of pollutants.

7. An example of the use of WSN in health applications is the Bi-Fi, embedded system architecture for patient monitoring in hospitals and out -patient care. It has been conceived at UCLA and is based on the SunSPOT architecture by Sun. The motes measure high-rate biological

data such as neural signals, pulse oximetry and electrocardiographs. The data is then interpreted, filtered, and transmitted by the motes to enable early warnings.

Roles in a Wireless Sensor Network

Nodes in a WSN can play different roles.

1. Sensor nodes are used to sense their surroundings and transmit the sensor readings to a sink node, also called "base station". They are typically equipped with different kinds of sensors. A mote is endowed with on-board processing, communication capabilities and sensing capabilities.

2. Sink nodes or "base stations" are tasked to collect the sensor readings of the other nodes and pass these readings to a gateway to which they are directly connected for further processing/analysis. A sink node is endowed with minimal on-board processing and communication capabilities but does not have sensing capabilities.

3. Actuators are devices which are used to control the environment, based on triggers revealed by the sensor readings or by other inputs. An actuator may have the same configuration as a mote but it is also endowed with controlling capabilities, for example to switch a light on under low luminosity.

Gateways often connected to sink nodes and are usually fed by a stable power supply since they consume considerable energy. These entities are normal computing devices such as laptops, notebooks, desktops, mobile phones or other emerging devices which are able to store, process and route the sensor readings to the processing place. However, they may not be endowed with sensing capabilities. Being range-limited, sensor motes require multi-hop communication capabilities to allow: 1) spanning distances much larger than the transmission range of a single node through localized communication between neighbor nodes 2) adaptation to network changes, for example, by routing around a failed node using a different path in order to improve performance and 3) using less transmitter power as a result of the shorter distance to be spanned by each node. They are deployed in three forms;

(1) Sensor node used to sense the environment.

(2) Relay node used as relay for the sensor readings received from other nodes and (3) Sink node also often called base station which is connected to a gateway (laptop, tablet, iPod, Smart phone, desktop) with higher energy budget capable of either processing the sensor readings locally or to transmit these readings to remote processing places.

Chapter 2.
Internet Principles

Introduction to IPv6

IPv6 stands for Internet Protocol version 6, so the importance of IPv6 is implicit in its name, it's as important as the Internet! The Internet Protocol (IP from now on) was intended as a solution to the need to interconnect different data networks, and has become the "de facto" standard for all kinds of digital communications. Nowadays IP is present in most devices that are able to send and receive digital information, not only the Internet.

IP is standardized by the IETF (Internet Engineering Task Force), the organization in charge of all the Internet standards, guaranteeing the interoperability among software from different vendors. The fact that IP is a standard is of vital importance, because today everything is getting connected to the Internet using IP. All common Operating Systems and networking libraries support IP to send and receive data. As part of this "everything-connected-to-Internet" is the IoT, so now you know why you are reading this chapter about IPv6, the last version of the Internet Protocol. In other words, today, the easiest way to send and receive data is by means of the standards used in the Internet, including IP.

A little bit of History

ARPAnet was the first attempt of the US Department of Defense (DoD) to devise a decentralized network more resilient to an attack, while able to interconnect completely different systems. ARPAnet was created in the seventies, but it was in 1983 when a brand new protocol stack was introduced, TCP/IP. The first widely used network protocol version was IPv4 (Internet Protocol version 4) which paved the way to the civilian Internet. Initially only research centers and universities were connected, supported by the NSF (National Science Foundation), and commercial applications where not allowed, but when the network started growing exponentially the NSF decided to transfer its operation and funding to private operators, lifting the restrictions to commercial traffic. While the main applications were email and file transfer, it was with the development of the World Wide Web based on the HTML protocol and specifically with the MOSAIC graphic interface browser and its successors that the traffic really exploded and the Internet began to be used by the masses. As a consequence there was a rapid depletion in the number of IP addresses available under IPv4, which was not designed to scale to these levels.

In order to allow for more addresses, you need a longer IP address space (greater number of bits to specify the address), which means a new architecture, which means changes to most of the routing and network software. After examining a number of proposals, the IETF settled on IPv6, described in the January 1995 RFC (Request for Comment, the official IETF documentation naming) 1752, sometimes also referred to as the Next Generation Internet Protocol, or IPng. The IETF updated the IPv6 standard in 1998 with the current definition covered in RFC 2460. By 2004, IPv6 was widely available from industry and supported by most new network equipment. Today IPv6 coexists with IPv4 in the Internet and the amount of IPv6 traffic is quickly growing as more and more ISPs and content providers have started supporting IPv6.

As you can see, the history of IP and Internet are almost the same, and because of this the growth of Internet is been hampered by the limitations of IPv4, and has led to the development of a new version of IP, IPv6, as the protocol to be used to interconnect all sorts of devices to send and/or receive information. There are even some technologies that are being developed only with IPv6 in mind, a good example in the context of the IoT is 6LowPAN.

From now on we will only center on IPv6. If you know something about IPv4, then you have half the way done, if not, don't worry we will cover the main concepts briefly and gently.

IPv6 Concepts

We will cover the the minimum you need to know about the last version of the Internet Protocol to understand why it's so useful for the IoT and how it's related with other protocols like 6LowPAN discussed later. We will assume that you are familiar with bits, bytes, networking stack, network layer, packets, IP header, etc. You should understand that IPv6 is a different protocol, non-compatible with IPv4.

In the following figure we represent the layered model used in the Internet.

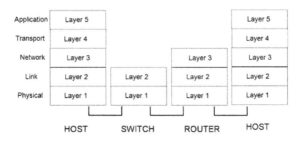

Figure 1.1. Internet Protocol stack

IPv6 sits in layer 3, called network layer. The pieces of data handled by layer 3 are called packets. Devices connected to the Internet can be hosts or routers. A host can be a PC, a laptop or a sensor board, sending and/or receiving data packets. Hosts will be the source or destination of the packets. Routers instead are in charge of packet forwarding, and are responsible of choosing the next router that will forward them towards the final destination. Internet is composed of a lot of interconnected routers, which receive data packets in one interface and send then as quick as possible using another interface towards another forwarding router.

IPv6 packet

The first thing you should know is what an IPv6 packet looks like. In the layered model we saw before, each layer introduces its own information in the packet, and this information is intended for, and can only be processed by the same layer in another IP device. This "conversation" between layers at the same level on different devices must follow a protocol.

The Internet layers are:

- **Application**: Here resides the software developed by programmers, that will use network services offered by the network stack. An example is the web browser that opens a network connection towards a web server. Another example is the web server software that runs in a server somewhere in the Internet waiting to answer request from client's browsers. Examples of application protocols are HTTP and DNS.

- **Transport**: Is a layer above the network layer that offers additional to it, for example, retransmission of lost packets or guaranteeing that the

22

packets are received in the same order they were sent. This layer will be the one that shows a "network service" to the application layer, a service they can use to send or receive data. TCP and UDP are the most common transport protocols used in Internet.

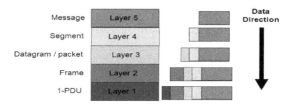

Figure 1.2. Data flow in the protocol stack

The bytes sent and received in the IP packet follow a standard format. The following figure shows the basic IPv6 header:

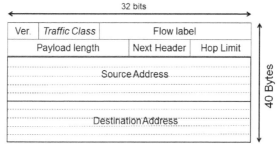

Figure 1.3. IPv6 Header

First you have the **basic IPv6 header** with a fixed size of 40 bytes, followed by upper layer data and optionally by some extension headers, which will be described later. As you can see there are several fields in the packet header, providing some improvements as compared with IPv4 header:

• The number of fields has been reduced from 12 to 8.

• The basic IPv6 header has a fixed size of 40 bytes and is aligned with 64 bits, allowing a faster hardware-based packet forwarding on routers.

• The size of addresses increased from 32 to 128 bits.

The most important fields are the source and destination addresses. As you already know, every IP device has a unique IP address that identifies it in the

23

Internet. This IP address is used by routers to take their forwarding decisions.

IPv6 header has 128 bits for each IPv6 address, this allows for 2^{128} addresses (approximately 3.4×10^{38}, i.e., 3.4 followed by 38 zeroes), whereas IPv4 uses 32 bits to encode each of the 2^{32} addresses (4,294,967,296) allowed.

We have seen the basic IPv6 header, and mentioned the **extension headers**. To keep the basic header simple and of a fixed size, additional features are added to IPv6 by means of extension headers.

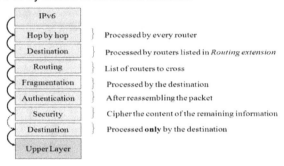

Figure 1.4. IPv6 Extension headers

Several extension headers have been defined, as you can see in the previous figure, and they have to follow the order shown. Extensions headers:

• Provide flexibility, for example, to enable security by ciphering the data in the packet.

• Optimize the processing of the packet, because with the exception of the hop by hop header, extensions are processed only by end nodes, (source and final destination of the packet), not by every router in the path.

• They are located as a "chain of headers" starting always in the basic IPv6 header, that use the field next header to point to the following extension header.

IPv6 addressing
1. The use of 128 bits for addresses brings some benefits:

- Provides many more addresses, to satisfy current and future needs, with ample space for innovation.
- Simplifies address auto-configuration mechanisms.
- Easier address management/delegation.
- Room for more levels of hierarchy and for route aggregation.
- Ability to do end-to-end IPsec.

IPv6 addresses are classified into the following categories (which also exist in IPv4): of four hexadecimal symbols, each group separated by a colon ":". The last two rules are for address notation compression, we will see how this works in the following.

Let's see some examples:

1) If we represent all the address bits we have the preferred form, for example:

2001:0db8:4004:0010:0000:0000:6543:0ffd

2) If we use squared brackets around the address we have the literal form of the address:

[2001:0db8:4004:0010:0000:0000:6543:0ffd]

3) If we apply the fourth rule, allowing compression within each group by eliminating leftmost zeroes, we have: 2001:db8:4004:10:0:0:6543:ffd

4) If we apply the fifth rule, allowing compression of one or more consecutive groups of zeroes using "::", we have: 2001:db8:4004:10::6543:ffd

Care should be taken when compressing and decompressing IPv6 addresses. The process should be reversible. It's very common to have some mistakes. For example, the following address 2001:db8:A:0:0:12:0:80 could be compressed even more using "::". we have two options:

a) 2001:db8:A::12:0:80 b) 2001:db8:A:0:0:12::80

Both are correct IPv6 addresses. But the address 2001:db8:A::12::80 is wrong, since it does not follow the last compression rule we saw above. The problem with this badly compressed address is that we can't be sure how to expand it, its ambiguous. We can't know if it expands to 2001:db8:A:0:12:0:0:80 or to 2001:db8:A:0:0:12:0:80 .

IPv6 network prefix

Last but not least you have to understand the concept of a **network prefix**, that indicates some fixed bits and some non-defined bits that could be used to create new sub-prefixes or to define complete IPv6 addresses assigned to hosts.
Let's see some examples:

1) The network prefix 2001:db8:1::/48 (the compressed form of

2001:0db8:0001:0000:0000:0000:0000:0000) indicates that the first 48 bits will always be the same (2001:0db8:0001) but that we can play with the
other 80 bits, for example, to obtain two smaller prefixes:
2001:db8:1:a::/64 and 2001:db8:1:b::/64 .

2) If we take one of the smaller prefixes defined above, 2001:db8:1:b::/64 , where the first 64 bits are fixed we have the rightmost 64 bits to assign, for example, to an IPv6 interface in a host: 2001:db8:1:b:1:2:3:4 . This last example allow us to introduce a basic concept in IPv6: * A /64 prefix is always used in a LAN (Local Area Network) . ***The rightmost 64 bits, are called the interface identifier (IID) because they uniquely identify a host's interface in the local network defined by the /64 prefix**. The following figure illustrates this statement:

Figure 1.6. Network and Interface ID

Now that you have seen your first IPv6 addresses we can enter into more detail about two types of addresses you will find when you start working with IPv6: reserved and unicast.

- The **unspecified address**, used as a placeholder when no address is available:

  0:0:0:0:0:0:0:0 (::/128)

- The **loopback address**, is used by a node to send an IPv6 packet to itself:

  0:0:0:0:0:0:0:1 (::1/128)

- **Documentation Prefix**: 2001:db8::/32 . This prefix is reserved to be used in examples and documentation, you have already seen it in this chapter.

As specified in [RFC6890] IANA maintains a registry of special purpose IPv6 addresses [IANA-IPV6-SPEC].

The following are some other types of unicast addresses [RFC4291]:

- **Link-local**: Link-local addresses are always present in an IPv6 interface that is connected to a network. They all start with the prefix FE80::/10 and can be used to communicate with other hosts on the same local network, i.e., all hosts connected to the same switch. They cannot be used to communicate with other networks, i.e., to send or receive packets through a router.

- **ULA** (Unique Local Address) [RFC4193]: All ULA addresses start with the prefix FC00::/7, which in practice means that you could see FC00::/8 or FD00::/8 . Intended for local communications, usually inside a single site, they are not expected to be routable on the global Internet but used only inside a more limited environment.

- **Global Unicast**: Equivalent to the IPv4 public addresses, they are unique in the whole Internet and can be used to send a packet from one site to any destination in Internet.

What is IPv6 used for?

As we have seen IPv6 has some features that facilitates things like global addressing and host's address autoconfiguration. Because IPv6 provides as many addresses as we may need for some hundreds of years, we can put a global unicast IPv6 address on almost anything we may think of. This brings back the initial Internet paradigm that every IP device could communicate with every IP device. This end-to-end communication allows bidirectional communication all over the Internet and between any IP device, which could result in collaborative applications and new ways of storing, sending and accessing the information.

In the context of this book we can, for example, contemplate IPv6 sensors all around the world collecting, sending and being accessed from different places to create a world-wide mesh of physical values measured, stored and processed.

The availability of a huge amount of addresses has allowed a new mechanism called **stateless address autoconfiguration** (SLAAC) that didn't exist with IPv4. Here is a brief summary of different ways to configure an address on an IPv6 interface:

- **Statically**: You can decide which address you will give to your IP device and then manually configure it into the device using any kind of interface: web, command line, etc. Normally you also have to configure other network parameters like the gateway to use to send packets out of your network.

- **DHCPv6** (Dynamic Host Configuration Protocol for IPv6) [RFC3315]: A porting of the similar mechanism already available in IPv4. You need to configure a dedicated server that after a brief negotiation with the device assigns an IP address to it. DHCPv6 allows IP devices to be configured automatically, this is why it is named as stateful address autoconfiguration, because the DHCPv6 server maintains a state of assigned addresses.

- **SLAAC**: Stateless address autoconfiguration [RFC4862] is a new mechanism introduced with IPv6 that allows to configure automatically all network parameters on an IP device using the router that gives connectivity to a network.

The advantage of SLAAC is that it simplifies the configuration of "dumb" devices, like sensors, cameras or any other device with low processing power. You don't need to use any interface in the IP device to configure anything, just "plug and net". It also simplifies the network infrastructure needed to build a basic IPv6 network, because you don't need additional device/ server, you use the same router you need to send packets outside your network to configure the IP devices. We are not going to enter into details, but you just need to know that in a LAN (Local Area Network), connected to Internet by means of a router, this router is in charge of sending all the configuration information needed to its hosts using an RA (Router Advertisement) message. The router will send RAs periodically, but in order to expedite the process a host can send an RS (Router Solicitation) message when its interface gets connected to the network. The router will send an RA immediately in response to the RS.

The following figure show the packet exchange between a host that has just connected to a local network and some IPv6 destination in the Internet:

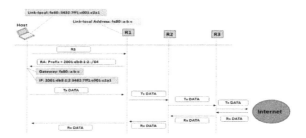

Figure 1.7. Packet exchange in IPv6

1) R1 is the router that gives connectivity to the host in the LAN and is periodically sending RAs.

2) Both R1 and Host have a link-local address in their interfaces connected to the host's LAN, this address is configured automatically when the interface is ready. Our host creates it's link-local address by combining the 64 leftmost bits of the link-local's prefix (fe80::/64) and the 64 rightmost bits of a locally generated IID (:3432:7ff1:c001:c2a1). These link-local addresses can be used in the LAN to exchange packets, but not to send packets outside the LAN.

3) The hosts needs two basic things to be able to send packets to other networks: a global IPv6 address and the address of a gateway, i.e., a router to which send the packets it wants to get routed outside its network.

4) Although R1 is sending RAs periodically (usually every several seconds) when the host get connected and has configured its link-local address, it sends an RS to which R1 responds immediately with an RA containing two

things:

1. A **global prefix of length 64 bits** that is intended for SLAAC. The host takes the received prefix and adds to it a locally generated IID, usually the same one used for link-local address. This way a global IPv6 address is configured in the host and now can communicate with the IPv6 Internet.

2. Implicitly included is the **link-local address of R1**, because it is the source address of the RA. Our host can use this address to configure the **default gateway**, the place to which send the packets by default, to reach an IPv6 host somewhere in Internet.

3. Once both the gateway and global IPv6 address are configured, the host can receive or
send information. In the figure it has something to send (Tx Data) to a host in Internet, so it
creates an IPv6 packet with the destination address of the recipient host and as source a
the just autoconfigured global address, which is sent to its gateway, R1's link-local address.
The destination host can answer with some data (Rx Data).

Network Example

Following we show how a simple IPv6 network looks like, displaying IPv6 addresses for all the networking devices.

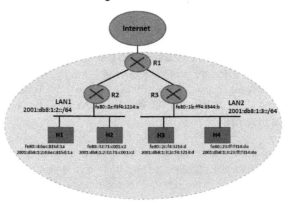

Figure 1.8. Simple IPv6 network

We have four hosts, (sensors, or other devices), and we want to put a pair of them in two different places, for example two floors in a building. We are dealing with four IP devices but you can have up to 2^{64} (18,446,744,073,709,551,616) devices connected on the same LAN.

We create two LANs with a router on each one, both routers connected to a central router (R1) that provides connectivity to Internet. LAN1 is served by R2 (with link-local address fe80::2c:f3f4:1214:a on that LAN) and uses the prefix 2001:db8:1:2::/64 announced by SLAAC. LAN2 is served by R3 (with link-local address fe80::1b:fff4:3344:b on that LAN) and uses the prefix 2001:db8:1:3::/64 announced by SLAAC.

All hosts have both a link-local IPv6 address and a global IPv6 address autoconfigured using the prefix provided by the corresponding router by means of RAs. In addition, remember that each host also configures the gateway using the link-local address used by the router for the RA. Link-local address can be used for communication among hosts inside a LAN, but for communicating with hosts in other LANs or any other network outside its own LAN a global IPv6 address is needed.

Short intro to Wireshark

Figure 1.9. Wireshark logo

Wireshark is a free and open-source packet analyzer, which allows packet traces to be sniffed, captured, and analyzed.

A packet trace is a record of traffic at some location on the network, as if a snapshot was taken of all the bits that passed across a particular wire. The packet trace records a timestamp for each packet, along with the bits that make up the packet, from the low-layer headers to the higher-layer contents.

Wireshark runs on most operating systems, including Windows, MAC and Linux. It provides a graphical user interface that shows the sequence of packets and the meaning of the bits when interpreted as protocol headers and data. The packets are color-coded to convey their meaning, and Wireshark includes various ways to filter and analyze them to let you investigate different aspects of behavior. It is widely used to troubleshoot networks.

A common usage scenario is when a person wants to troubleshoot network problems or look at the internal workings of a network protocol. A user could, for example, see exactly what happens when he or she opens up a website or sets up a wireless sensor network. It is also possible to filter and search for given packet attributes, which facilitates the debugging process.

More information and installation instructions are available at Wireshark site..

Figure 1.10. Wireshark Screenshot

When you open Wireshark, there are four main areas, from top to bottom: menus and filters, list of captured packets, detailed information about the selected packet, including its full content in hexadecimal and ASCII. Online directly links you to the Wiresharks site, where you can find a handy user guide and information on the security of Wireshark. Under Files, you'll find Open, which lets you open previously captured files,, and Sample Captures. You can download any of the sample captures through this website, and study the data. This will help you understand what kind of packets Wireshark can capture.

The Capture section let you choose your Interface from the available ones. It'll also show you which ones are active. Clicking details will show you some pretty generic information about that interface.

32

Under Start, you can choose one or more interfaces to check out. Capture Options allows you to customize what information you see during a capture. Here you can choose a filter, a capture file, and more. Under Capture Help, you can read up on how to capture, and you can check info on Network Media about which interfaces work on which platforms.

Let's select an interface and click Start. To stop a capture, press the red square in the top toolbar. If you want to start a new capture, hit the green triangle which looks like a shark fin next to it. Now that you have got a finished capture, you can click File, and save, open, or merge the capture. You can print it, you can quit the program, and you can export your packet capture in a variety of ways.

You can find a certain packet, copy packets, mark (highlight) any specific packet or all the packets. Another interesting thing you can do under Edit, is resetting the time value. You'll notice that the time is in seconds incrementing. You can reset it from the packet you've clicked on. You can add a comment to a packet, configure profiles and preferences.

When we select a packet from the list of captured ones, Wireshark shows detailed information of the different protocols used by that packet, for example Ethernet:

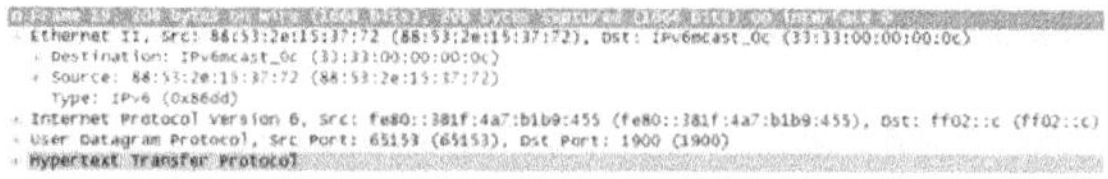

Figure 1.11. Ethernet packet

Or IPv6, where we can see the fields we mentioned before: Version, Traffic class, flowlabel, payload length, next header, etc.:

Figure 1.12. IPv6 packet

There are two methods to apply filters to the list of captured packets:

- Write a filter expression on the specific box and then apply it. Protocols can be specified (ip,ipv6, icmp, icmpv6), fields of a protocol (ipv6.dst, ipv6.src) and even complex expressions can be created using operators like AND (&&), OR (||) or the negation (|).

Figure 1.13. Wireshark Filter

- Another option to create filters is to right click in one filed of a captured packet, in the list of captured packets. There will appear a menu option "Apply as filter", with several options on how to use that field.

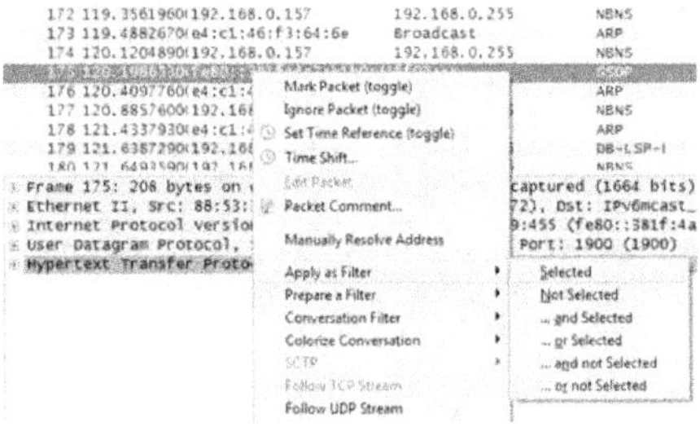

Figure 1.14. Wireshark Captured packets

Another useful and interesting option of Wireshark is the possibility to see statistics about the captured traffic. If we have applied filters, the statistics will be about the filtered traffic. Just go to the Statistics menu and select, for example, Protocol Hierarchy:

Figure 1.15. Wireshark statistics

Other interesting options are:

- Conversation List → IPv6
- Statistics → Endpoint List → IPv6
- Statistics → IO Graph

This last option allow to create graphs with different lines for different types of traffic and save the image:

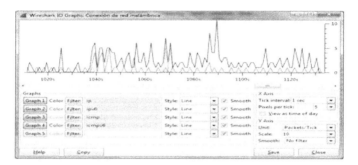

Figure 1.16. Wireshark charts

Connecting our IPv6 Network to the Internet

As said in the introduction of this book, network communications is one of the four basic elements of an IoT system. We already have seen that IPv6 brings the possibility of giving an IP address to almost anything we can think of, and can do this making it easy to autoconfigure network parameters on our devices.

Once we have all our "things" connected using IPv6, they can use it to communicate among them locally or with any other "thing" on the IPv6 Internet. In this chapter we will **focus on the Internet side of the communication of the "things"** composing the Internet of Things.

As we will see in this book, the capability of connecting our devices to the Internet allows new possibilities and services. For example, we can connect our wireless sensors networks to a centralized repository, where all the sensed information can be processed and stored for historical records, which will uncover underlying patterns and maybe predict future events. This basic idea is what nowadays is called "Big Data" and has a whole set of its own concepts and techniques.

35

Wireless IoT Communication Protocols

IoT involves smart devices available in the entire region and networked them as personal wireless network locally and worldwide through the Internet. wireless communication technologies required for connectivity. Some main protocols are Bluetooth, Wi-Fi, ZigBee, Z-Wave and RF Link. In IOT implementation Communication Technologies utilized by IoT devices are summarized below:

i. ZigBee

This ZigBee standard defines the physical and Medium Access Control layers for cheap wireless networks [3]. The physical layer Zigbee functions are channel selection, link quality, energy measurement and channel assessment. For the network and the application layer, ZigBee standard is applicable. The network layer provides routing over the internet, specifying different network topologies: star, tree, peer-to-peer and mesh. In the application layer provides a framework for distributed application development and communication. Zigbee is used in agriculture and food industry, additionally used in a smart home, automation, security, and medical monitoring. [4]

ii. RF Links

RF communication modules data rates are quite low ranges up to 1Mpbs and also need an Internet-enabled gateway that will provide access to the devices for making a complete IoT network. The Radio Frequency Identification (RFID) technology has been initially introduced for identifying and tracking objects with the help of small electronic chips, called tags. RFID has been originally categorized as the enabling communication power for the Internet of Things, due to its low cost, high mobility, and efficiency in identifying devices and objects. Despite RFID is very common for device identification and some information exchange [5]

iii. Bluetooth

Bluetooth (IEEE 802.15.1) is a wireless protocol for short-range communication in wireless personal area networks (PAN) as a cable replacement for mobile devices. It uses the 2.4 GHz radio bands to communicate at 1 Mb per second between up to seven devices. Bluetooth is low-powered devices to use for small data like health or tracker. When connectivity is initiated Bluetooth comes into action from sleep mode and conserves power. It uses a method of frequency-hopping spread-spectrum (FHSS) communication, transmits data over different frequencies at different time intervals. Bluetooth uses a master-slave-based MAC (medium access control) protocol [6-8]

iv. 6LoWPAN

The 6LoWPAN is Wireless PAN with low power, large-scale network and supports IPv6. It is a connection-oriented technology in which router forwards the data to its next hop to the 6LoWPAN gateway which is connected to 6LoWPAN with the IPv6 domain and then forwards the data to its respected device correctly. With IPv6 we have enough address space to identify all the things in the world. In IP based network standard protocols (HTTP, TCP/IP) are directly applied to sensor nodes just as they do with traditional web servers out there on the Internet [9][10].

v. Z-Wave

Z-Wave protocol architecture is low power consuming mostly used in home automation, security and light commercial environment. It has an open communication protocol. The main purpose of Z-wave is a reliable mesh network, message passing from a control unit to one or more nodes in the network. Z-wave have two types of devices, one is poll Controllers which send commands to the slaves, the second type of device, which replies to the controller to execute the commands.

vi.Wi-Fi Wireless fidelity

Wireless fidelity is known as Wi-Fi, with the IEEE 802.11x standards, common way to connect devices wirelessly to the Internet. Laptop, Smartphone, and Tablet PC are equipped with Wi-Fi interfaces and talk to a wireless router and provide two-way accesses to the Internet. The Wi-Fi standard family allows establishing a wireless network on short distances. Wi-Fi has series types of networks of IEEE 802.11 and IEEE security extension. The Wi-Fi group is working on an unlicensed spectrum of 2.4 GHz band. WIFI consumes more power. [13-14]

TECHNOLOGY STACK

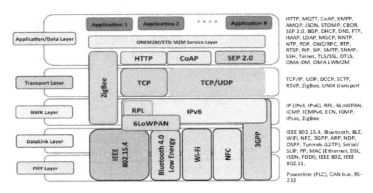

Figure: IOT research EU

MQTT - Message Queue Telemetry Transport
It is a publish subscribe based lightweight messaging protocol for use in conjunction with the TCP/IP protocol. This provides an embedded connection from applications to a middleware's on one side. on the other

side connection from networks to communications, The system consists of three main components: publishers, subscribers, and an agent. MQTT enters in sleep mode once data transmission complete.

CoAP - Constrained Application Protocol

CoAP designed for small devices, Machine to Machine, low powered applications such as smart energy and building automation.Request-Response based model for end-points using Client-Server interaction is asynchronous over a datagram-oriented transport protocol such as UDP.

XMPP – Extensible Messaging and Presence Protocol

Extensible Messaging and Presence Protocol (XMPP) is a messaging protocol is a highly efficient protocol over the internet. XMPP supports both publish/ subscribe and request/ response architecture and it is up to the application developer to choose which architecture to use. Real-time application and M2M can be implemented using XMPP having low latency.

38

Data Handling in IOT

Data management in IOT is at various levels is handled by

- Sensor
- Sensor cloud (FoG)
- Cloud

Cloud model cannot store all these IOT data. Data need to be filtered. The ability of the current cloud model is insufficient to handle the requirements of IoT. Issues are: Volume, Latency, and Bandwidth

Volume: The total number of connected vehicles worldwide will be 250 million by 2020. There will be more than 30 billion IoT devices. The amount of data generated by IoT devices is simply huge. Private firms, Factories, airplane companies' produce colossus amount of data every day.

Latency: Latency is time taken by a data packet of a round trip. Latency is an important aspect of handing a time-sensitive data. If edge devices send time-sensitive data to the cloud for analysis and wait for the cloud to give a proper action, then it can lead to many unwanted results. While handling time-sensitive data, a millisecond can make huge differences. Reduce latency of data and appropriate actions at the right time prevent major accidents machine failure etc. A minute delay while taking a decision makes a huge difference. Latency can be reduced by analyzing the data close to the data source

Bandwidth: Bandwidth is bit-rate of data during transmission. If all the data generated by IoT devices are sent to cloud for storage and analysis, then, the traffic generated by these devices will be simply enormous, consumes almost all the bandwidths. Handling this kind of traffic will be simply a very hard task.

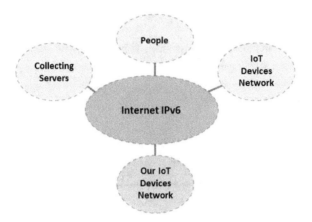

Figure 1.18. IPv6 Connectivity

Getting back to the network connectivity domain, our objective is to connect IoT devices to the Internet using IPv6, allowing communication with other IoT devices, collecting servers or even with people.

Related with the IPv6 connectivity to Internet is an important idea: **communication between IoT devices and the IPv6 Internet could be bidirectional**. This is important to remark because with IPv4, connectivity is oftentimes designed as a one direction channel between a client and a server. This changes with IPv6.

Having a bidirectional communication with the IoT devices allows useful possibilities, because its not just that the device can send information to somewhere in the Internet, but that anybody in the Internet could be able to send information, requests or commands to the IoT device. This can be used in different scenarios:

- **Management**: To manage the IoT device performing some status tests, updating some parameters/configuration/firmware remotely allowing for a better and efficient use of the hardware platform and improving the infrastructure security.

- **Control**: Send commands or control actuators to make the IoT device perform an action.

- **Communication**: Send information to the IoT device, that can be displayed

40

using some kind of interface.

IIPv6 is still being deployed all over the different networks that compose the Internet, which means that different scenarios can be found when deciding how to connect our network to the IPv6 Internet. Following are the three most common scenarios, in preferred order, being Native IPv6 connectivity the best choice.

• **Native IPv6 Connectivity**: This scenario applies when both the ISP providing connectivity to the Internet and the router(s) and networks devices used in our network support of IPv6. Native IPv6 means that the IPv6 packets will flow without being changed or tunnelled anywhere in its path from origin to destination. It is common to find what is called dual-stack networks, where both native IPv6 and native IPv4 are being used at the same time in the same interfaces and devices. This native IPv6 scenario covers both cases: IPv6-only and dual-stack.

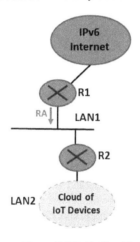

Figure 1.19. Native IPv6

As seen in the figure, our IoT devices cloud is connected to a router (R2) that provides them a prefix creating a LAN (LAN2). The router that provides connectivity to the IPv6 Internet (R1) will also be in charge of autoconfiguring IPv6 devices in LAN1 (including R2), by sending RAs (Router Advertisements) as detailed when SLAAC was explained.

• **No IPv6 connectivity**: In this scenario we face a common problem nowadays, the lack of IPv6 connectivity from an ISP. Although we have IPv6 support on the router that connects our network to Internet, the ISP supports only IPv4. The solution is to use one of the so called IPv6 Transition Mechanism. The most simple and useful in this case would be the 6in4 tunnel, based on creating a point-to-point static tunnel that encapsulates IPv6 packets into IPv4.

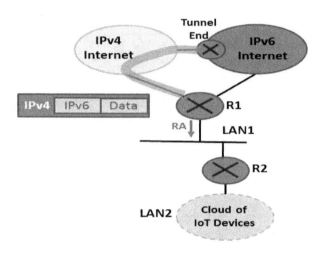

Figure 1.20. IPv4 tunneled IPv6

The figure shows this solution created by making a tunnel from R1 to a "remote tunnel end point" where the IPv4 meets the IPv6 Internet. This will be a router having connectivity to both the IPv4 and IPv6 Internet. The native IPv6 traffic from our networks (LAN1 and LAN2) will reach R1, which will take the whole IPv6 packet with its data, and put it inside a new IPv4 packet with the IPv4 destination address corresponding to the tunnel end router. The tunnel end router will grab the IPv6 packet and convey it as native IPv6 traffic into the IPv6 Internet. Similar encapsulation is applied with the IPv6 traffic sent over Ipv4 from the IPv6 Internet to our networks

No IPv6 connectivity and no IPv6 capable router: This scenario covers the case where there is no IPv6 connectivity from the ISP, nor IPv6 support on the router connecting our network to the Internet. As seen before, to solve the lack of IPv6 connectivity from the ISP we can use a 6in4 tunnel, but in this scenario we also have to face the lack of IPv6 support on the router which prevents the creation of the tunnel. The solution is to add a new router that supports both IPv6 and IPv4, and create a 6in4 tunnel from this router to a tunnel end router somewhere on the IPv4 Internet.

Chapter 3.
Introduction to 6LoWPAN

One of the drivers of the IoT, where anything can be connected, is the use of wireless technologies to create a communication channel to send and receive information. This wide adoption of wireless technologies allows increasing the number of connected devices but results in limitations in terms of cost, battery life, power consumption, and communication distance for the devices. New technologies and protocols should tackle a new environment, usually called Low power and Lossy networks (LLNs), with the following characteristics:

1. Significantly more devices than those on current local area networks.

2. Severely limited code and ram space in devices.

3. Networks with limited communications distance (range), power and processing resources.

4. All elements should work together to optimize energy consumption and bandwidth usage.

Another factor that is being widely adopted within IoT is the use of IP as the network protocol. The use of IP provides several advantages, because it is an open standard that is widely available, allowing for easy and cheap adoption, good interoperability and easy application layer development. The use of a common standard like an end-to-end IP-based solution avoids the problem of non-interoperable networks.

For wireless communication technology, the IEEE 802.15.4 standard [IEEE802.15.4] is very promising for the lower (link and physical) layers, although others are also being considered as good options like Low Power WiFi, Bluetooth ® Low Energy, DECT Ultra Low Energy, ITU-T G.9959 networks, and NFC (Near Field Communication).

One component of the IoT that has received significant support from vendors and standardization organizations is that of WSN (Wireless Sensor Networks).
The IETF has different working groups (WGs) developing standards to be used by WSN:

1. **6lowpan**: IPv6 over Low-power Wireless Personal Area Networks [sixlowpan], defines the standards for IPv6 communication over the IEEE 802.15.4 wireless communication technology. 6lowpan acts as an adaptation layer between the standard IPv6 world and the low power and lossy wireless communications medium offered by IEEE 802.15.4. Note that this standard is only defined with IPv6 in mind, no IPv4 support is available.

2. **roll**: Routing Over Low power and Lossy networks [roll]. LLNs have specific routing requirements that could not be satisfied with existing routing protocols. This WG

focuses on routing solutions for a subset of all possible application areas of LLNs (industrial, connected
home, building and urban sensor networks), and protocols are designed to satisfy their application-specific routing requirements. Here again the WG focuses only on the IPv6 routing architectural framework.

3. **6lo**: IPv6 over Networks of Resource-constrained Nodes [sixlo]. This WG deals with IPv6 connectivity over constrained node networks. It extends the work of the 6lowpan WG, defining IPv6-over-foo adaptation layer specifications using 6LoWPAN for link layer in constrained node networks.

As seen, 6LoWPAN is the basis of the work carried out in standardization at IETF to communicate constrained resources nodes in LLNs using IPv6. The work on 6LoWPAN has been completed and is being further complemented by the roll WG to satisfy routing needs and the 6lo WG to extend the 6lowpan standards to any other link layer technology. Following are more details about 6LoWPAN, as the first step into the IPv6 based WSN/IoT. 6LoWPAN and related standards are concerned about providing IP connectivity to devices, irrelevantly of the upper layers, except for the UDP transport layer protocol that is specifically considered.

Overview of LoWPANs

Low-power and lossy networks (LLNs) is the term commonly used to refer to networks made of highly constrained nodes (limited CPU, memory, power) interconnected by a variety of "lossy" links (low-power radio links). They are characterized by low speed, low performance, low cost, and unstable connectivity.

A LoWPAN is a particular instance of an LLN, formed by devices complying with the IEEE 802.15.4 standard.

The typical characteristics of devices in a LoWPAN are:

1. **Limited Processing Capability**: Different types and clock speeds processors, starting at 8-bits.
2. **Small Memory Capacity**: From few kilobytes of RAM with a few dozen kilobytes of ROM/ flash memory, it's expected to grow in the future, but always trying to keep at the minimum necessary.

3. **Low Power**: In the order of tens of milliamperes.

4. **Short Range**: The Personal Operating Space (POS) defined by IEEE 802.15.4 implies a range of 10 meters. For real implementations it can reach over 100 meters in line-of-sight situations.

5. **Low Cost**: This drives some of the other characteristics such as low processing, low memory, etc.

All this constraints on the nodes are expected to change as technology evolves, but compared to other fields it's expected that the LoWPANs will always try to use very restricted devices to allow for low prices and long life which implies hard restrictions in all other features.

A LoWPAN typically includes devices that work together to connect the physical environment to real-world applications, e.g., wireless sensors, although a LoWPAN is not necessarily comprised of sensor nodes only, since it may also contain actuators.

It's also important to identify the characteristics of LoWPANs, because they will be the constraints guiding all the technical work:

1. Small packet size: Given that the maximum physical layer frame is 127 bytes, the resulting maximum frame size at the media access control layer is 102 octets. Link-layer security imposes further overhead, which leaves a maximum of 81 octets for data packets.

2. IEEE 802.15.4 defines several addressing modes: It allows the use of either IEEE 64-bit extended addresses or (after an association event) 16-bit addresses unique within the PAN (Personal Area Network).

3. Low bandwidth: Data rates of 250 kbps, 40 kbps, and 20 kbps for each of the currently defined physical layers (2.4GHz, 915MHz, and 868MHz, respectively).

4. Topologies include star and mesh.

5. Large number of devices expected to be deployed during the lifetime of the technology. Location of the devices is typically not predefined, as they tend to be deployed in an ad-hoc fashion. Sometimes the location of these devices may not be easily accessible or they may move to new locations.

a. The pervasive nature of IP networks allows leveraging existing infrastructure.

b. IP-based technologies already exist, are well-known, proven to be working and widely available. This allows for an easier and cheaper adoption, good interoperability and easier application layer development.

c. IP networking technology is specified in open and freely available specifications, which is able to be better understood by a wider audience than proprietary solutions.

d. Tools for IP networks already exist.

e. IP-based devices can be connected readily to other IP-based networks, without the need for intermediate entities like protocol translation gateways or proxies.

f. The use of IPv6, specifically, allows for a huge amount of addresses and provides for easy network parameters autoconfiguration (SLAAC). This is paramount for 6LoWPANs where large number of devices should be supported.

On the counter side using IP communication in LoWPANs raise some issues that should be taken into account:

a. IP Connectivity: One of the characteristics of 6LoWPANs is the limited packet size, which implies that headers for IPv6 and layers above must be compressed whenever possible.

b. Topologies: LoWPANs must support various topologies including mesh and star: Mesh topologies imply multi-hop routing to a desired destination. In this case, intermediate devices act as packet forwarders at the link layer. Star topologies include provisioning a subset of devices with packet forwarding functionality. If, in addition to IEEE 802.15.4, these devices use other kinds of network interfaces such as Ethernet or IEEE 802.11, the goal is to seamlessly integrate the networks built over those different technologies. This, of course, is a primary motivation to use IP to begin with.

c. Limited Packet Size: Applications within LoWPANs are expected to originate small packets. Adding all layers for IP connectivity should still allow transmission in one frame, without incurring excessive fragmentation and reassembly. Furthermore, protocols must be designed or chosen so that the individual "control/protocol packets" fit within a single 802.15.4 frame.

d. Limited Configuration and Management: Devices within LoWPANs are expected to be deployed in exceedingly large numbers. Additionally, they are expected to have limited display and input capabilities. Furthermore, the location of some of these devices may be hard to reach. Accordingly, protocols used in LoWPANs should have minimal configuration, preferably work "out of the box", be easy to bootstrap, and enable the network to self heal given the inherent unreliable characteristic of these devices.

e. Service Discovery: LoWPANs require simple service discovery network protocols to discover, control and maintain services provided by devices.

f. Security: IEEE 802.15.4 mandates link-layer security based on AES, but it omits any details about topics like bootstrapping, key management, and security at higher layers. Of course, a complete security solution for LoWPAN devices must consider application needs very carefully.

6LoWPAN

We have seen that there is a lower layer (physical and link layers on TCP/IP stack model) that provide connectivity to devices in what is called a LoWPAN. Also that using IPv6 over this layer would bring several benefits. The main reason for developing the IETF standards mentioned in the introduction is that between the IP (network layer) and the lower layer there are some important issues that need to be solved by means of an adaptation layer, the 6lowpan.

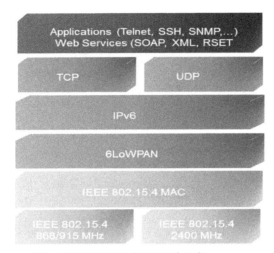

Figure 2.1. 6LoWPAN in the protocol stack

The main goals of 6lowpan are:

1. Fragmentation and Reassembly layer: IPv6 specification [RFC2460] establishes that the minimum MTU that a link layer should offer to the IPv6 layer is 1280 bytes. The protocol data units may be as small as 81 bytes in IEEE 802.15.4. To solve this difference a fragmentation and reassembly adaptation layer must be provided at the layer below IP.

2. Header Compression: Given that in the worst case the maximum size available for transmitting IP packets over an IEEE 802.15.4 frame is 81 octets, and that the IPv6 header is 40 octets long, (without optional extension headers), this leaves only 41 octets for upper-layer protocols, like UDP and TCP. UDP uses 8 octets in the header and TCP uses 20 octets. This leaves 33 octets for data over UDP and 21 octets for data over TCP. Additionally, as pointed above, there is also a need for a fragmentation and reassembly layer, which will use even more octets leaving very few octets for data. Thus, if one were to use the protocols as is, it would lead to excessive fragmentation and reassembly, even when data packets are just 10s of octets long. This points to the need for header compression.

3. Address Autoconfiguration: specifies methods for creating IPv6 stateless address auto configuration (in contrast to stateful) that is attractive for 6LoWPANs, because it reduces the configuration overhead on the hosts. There is a need for a method to generate the IPv6 IID (Interface Identifier) from the EUI-64 assigned to the IEEE 802.15.4 device.

4. Mesh Routing Protocol: A routing protocol to support a multi-hop mesh network is necessary. Care should be taken when using existing routing protocols (or designing new ones) so that the routing packets fit within a single IEEE 802.15.4 frame. The mechanisms defined by 6lowpan IETF WG are based on some requirements for the IEEE 802.15.4 layer:

5. IEEE 802.15.4 defines four types of frames: beacon frames, MAC command frames, acknowledgement frames and data frames. IPv6 packets must be carried on data frames.

6. Data frames may optionally request that they be acknowledged. It is recommended that IPv6 packets be carried in frames for which acknowledgements are requested so as to aid link-layer recovery.

7. The specification allows for frames in which either the source or destination addresses (or both) are elided. Both source and destination addresses are required to be included in the IEEE 802.15.4 frame header.

8. The source or destination PAN ID fields may also be included. 6LoWPAN standard assumes that a PAN maps to a specific IPv6 link.

9. Both 64-bit extended addresses and 16-bit short addresses are supported, although additional constraints are imposed on the format of the 16-bit short addresses.

10. Multicast is not supported natively in IEEE 802.15.4. Hence, IPv6 level multicast packets must be carried as link-layer broadcast frames in IEEE 802.15.4 networks. This must be done such that the broadcast frames are only heeded by devices within the specific PAN of the link in question.

The 6LoWPAN adaptation format was specified to carry IPv6 datagrams over constrained links, taking into account limited bandwidth, memory, or energy resources that are expected in applications such as wireless sensor networks. For each of these goals and requirements there is a solution provided by the 6lowpan specification:

1. A Mesh Addressing header to support sub-IP forwarding.

2. A Fragmentation header to support the IPv6 minimum MTU requirement.

3. A Broadcast Header to be used when IPv6 multicast packets must be sent over the IEEE 802.15.4 network.

4. Stateless header compression for IPv6 datagrams to reduce the relatively large IPv6 and UDP headers down to (in the best case) several bytes. These header are used as the LoWPAN encapsulation, and could be used at the same time forming what is called the header stack. Each header in the header stack contains a header type followed by zero or more header fields. When more than one LoWPAN header is used in the same packet, they must appear in the following order: Mesh Addressing

Header, Broadcast Header, and Fragmentation Header.

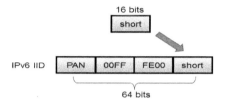

Figure 2.2. 6LoWPAN headers

IPv6 Interface Identifier (IID)

As already said an IEEE 802.15.4 device could have two types of addresses. For each one 5there is a different way of generating the IPv6 IID.

1. IEEE EUI-64 address: All devices have this one. In this case, the Interface Identifier is formed from the EUI-64, complementing the "Universal/Local" (U/L) bit, which is the next-to-lowest order bit of the first octet of the EUI-64. Complementing this bit will generally change a 0 value to a 1.

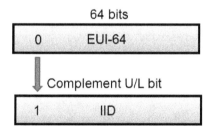

Figure 2.3. EUI-64 derived IID

1. 16-bit short addresses: Possible but not always used. The IPv6 IID is formed using the PAN (or zeroes in case of not knowing the PAN) and the 16 bit short address as in the figure below.

Header Compression

Two encoding formats are defined for compression of IPv6 packets: LOWPAN_IPHC and LOWPAN_NHC, an encoding format for arbitrary next headers.

To enable effective compression, LOWPAN_IPHC relies on information pertaining to the entire 6LoWPAN. LOWPAN_IPHC assumes the following will be the common case for 6LoWPAN communication:

1. Version is 6.

2. Traffic Class and Flow Label are both zero.

3. Payload Length can be inferred from lower layers from either the 6LoWPAN Fragmentation header or the IEEE 802.15.4 header.

4. Hop Limit will be set to a well-known value by the source.

5. Addresses assigned to 6LoWPAN interfaces will be formed using the link-local prefix or a small set of routable prefixes assigned to the entire 6LoWPAN.

6. Addresses assigned to 6LoWPAN interfaces are formed with an IID derived directly from either the 64-bit extended or the 16-bit short IEEE 802.15.4 addresses. Depending on how closely the packet matches this common case, different fields may not be compressible thus needing to be carried "in-line" as well. The base format used in LOWPAN_IPHC encoding is shown in the figure below.

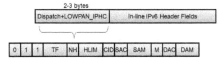

Figure 2.5. Header compression

Where:

- TF: Traffic Class, Flow Label.
- NH: Next Header.
- HLIM: Hop Limit.
- CID: Context Identifier Extension.
- SAC: Source Address Compression.
- SAM: Source Address Mode.
- M: Multicast Compression.
- DAC: Destination Address Compression.
- DAM: Destination Address Mode.

Not going into details, it's important to understand how 6LoWPAN compression works. To this end, let's see two examples:

1. HLIM (Hop Limit): Is a two bits field that can have four values, three of them make the hop limit field to be compressed from 8 to 2 bits:

a. 00: Hop Limit field carried in-line. There is no compression and the whole field is carried in-line after the LOWPAN_IPHC.

b. 01: Hop Limit field compressed and the hop limit is 1.

c. 10: Hop Limit field compressed and the hop limit is 64.

d. 11: Hop Limit field compressed and the hop limit is 255.

2. SAC/DAC used for the source IPv6 address compression. SAC indicates which address compression is used, stateless (SAC=0) or stateful context-based (SAC=1). Depending on SAC, DAC is used in the following way:

   a. If SAC=0, then SAM:

   - 00: 128 bits. Full address is carried in-line. No compression.

   - 01: 64 bits. First 64-bits of the address are elided, the link-local prefix. The remaining 64 bits are carried in-line.

   - 10: 16 bits. First 112 bits of the address are elided. First 64 bits is the link-local prefix. The following 64 bits are 0000:00ff:fe00:XXXX, where XXXX are the 16 bits carried in-line.

   - 11: 0 bits. Address is fully elided. First 64 bits of the address are the link-local prefix. The remaining 64 bits are computed from the encapsulating header (e.g., 802.15.4 or IPv6 source address).

   b. If SAC=1, then SAM:

   - 00: 0 bits. The unspecified address (::).

   - 01: 64 bits. The address is derived using context information and the 64 bits carried in-line. Bits covered by context information are always used. Any IID bits not covered by context information are taken directly from the corresponding bits carried in-line.

   - 10: 16 bits. The address is derived using context information and the 16 bits carried in-line. Bits covered by context information are always used. Any IID bits not covered by context information are taken directly from their corresponding bits in the 16-bit
   to IID mapping given by 0000:00ff:fe00:XXXX, where XXXX are the 16 bits carried in-line.
   - 11: 0 bits. The address is fully elided and it is derived using context information and the encapsulating header (e.g., 802.15.4 or IPv6 source address). Bits covered by context information are always used. Any IID bits not covered by context information are computed from the encapsulating header.

The base format is two bytes (16 bits) long. If the CID (Context Identifier Extension) field has a value of 1, it means that an additional 8-bit Context Identifier Extension field immediately follows the Destination Address Mode (DAM) field. This would make the length be 24 bits or three bytes.

This additional octet identifies the pair of contexts to be used when the IPv6 source and/or destination address is compressed. The context identifier is 4 bits for each address, supporting up to 16 contexts. Context 0 is the default context. The two fields on the Context Identifier Extension are:

• SCI: Source Context Identifier. Identifies the prefix that is used when the IPv6 source address is statefully compressed.
• DCI: Destination Context Identifier. Identifies the prefix that is used when the IPv6 destination address is statefully compressed.

The Next Header field in the IPv6 header is treated in two different ways, depending on the values indicated in the NH (Next Header) field of the LOWPAN_IPHC encoding shown above.

If NH = 0, then this field is not compressed and all the 8 bits are carried in-line after the LOWPAN_IPHC.

If NH = 1, then the Next Header field is compressed and the next header is encoded using LOWPAN_NHC encoding. This results in the structure shown in the figure below.

Figure 2.6. LoWPAN header

For IPv6 Extension headers the LOWPAN_NHC has the format shown in the figure, where:
• EID: IPv6 Extension Header ID:
   ◦ 0: IPv6 Hop-by-Hop Options Header.
   ◦ 1: IPv6 Routing Header.
   ◦ 2: IPv6 Fragment Header.
   ◦ 3: IPv6 Destination Options Header.
   ◦ 4: IPv6 Mobility Header.
   ◦ 5: Reserved.
   ◦ 6: Reserved.
   ◦ 7: IPv6 Header.

• NH: Next Header

- 0: Full 8 bits for Next Header are carried in-line.
- 1: Next Header field is elided and is encoded using LOWPAN_NHC. For the most part, the IPv6 Extension Header is carried unmodified in the bytes immediately following the LOWPAN_NHC octet.

NDP optimization

IEEE 802.15.4 and other similar link technologies have limited or no usage of multicast signalling due to energy conservation. In addition, the wireless network may not strictly follow the traditional concept of IP subnets and IP links. IPv6 Neighbor Discovery was not designed for non-transitive wireless links, since its reliance on the traditional IPv6 link concept and its heavy use of multicast make it inefficient and sometimes impractical in a low-power and lossy network.

For this reasons, some simple optimizations have been defined for IPv6 Neighbor Discovery, its addressing mechanisms and duplicate address detection for LoWPANs [RFC6775]:

1. Host-initiated interactions to allow for sleeping hosts.

2. Elimination of multicast-based address resolution for hosts.

3. A host address registration feature using a new option in unicast Neighbor Solicitation (NS) and Neighbor Advertisement (NA) messages.

4. A new Neighbor Discovery option to distribute 6LoWPAN header compression context to hosts.

5. Multi-hop distribution of prefix and 6LoWPAN header compression context.

6. Multi-hop Duplicate Address Detection (DAD), which uses two new ICMPv6 message types.

The two multi-hop items can be substituted by a routing protocol mechanism if that is desired.
Three new ICMPv6 message options are defined:
1. The Address Registration Option (ARO).

2. The Authoritative Border Router Option (ABRO).

3. The 6LoWPAN Context Option (6CO)

Also two new ICMPv6 message types are defined:
1. The Duplicate Address Request (DAR).

2. The Duplicate Address Confirmation (DAC)

Chapter 4.
Embedded Devices

YOU HAVE AN idea for a *thing*, and you know that it has some sort of interactive or electronic side to it. What is the first step in turning that from a vision in your head into something in the real world?

You likely can try out a number of different parts of the behaviour in isolation, and that's a good starting point for your initial prototype. After you do some research on the Internet to find similar projects or look through the catalogues of component retailers, such as RS (www.rs-components.com/) or Farnell (www.farnell. com/), you'll have a list of possible components and modules which might let you achieve your goal.

The more you dabble in electronics and microcontrollers, the bigger your collection of spare parts and leftovers from previous projects will grow. When you sit down to try out some of your ideas, either you'll have rooted through your collection for parts which are close enough to those you identified in your research, or you'll have an assortment of freshly purchased components. Usually, it's a combination of the two.

That's the typical decider when first trying out an idea: you use what's easily to hand, partly because it's generally something you're familiar with already but also because it helps keep the costs down. Even if you know that the board you're using won't be the ideal fit for a final version, if it lets you try out some of the functionality more quickly or more cheaply, that can mean it's the right choice for now.

One of the main areas where something vastly overpowered, and in theory much more expensive, can be the right choice for prototyping is using a mobile phone, laptop, or desktop computer to develop the initial software. If you already have a phone or computer which you can use, using it for your prototype isn't actually any more expensive.

However, if you haven't been playing around with electronics already and don't have a collection of development boards gathering dust in your desk drawer, how do you choose which one to buy? In this chapter, we explain some of the differences and features of a number of popular options. Over time the list will change, but you should still be able to work out how the same criteria we discussed in the preceding chapter apply to whichever boards you are considering.

This chapter starts with a look at electronics because whatever platform you end up choosing, the rest of the circuitry that you will build to connect it to will be pretty much the same. Then we choose four different platforms that you could use as a basis for your Internet of Things prototype. They aren't the only options, but they cover the breadth of options available. By the end of the chapter you will have a good feel for the trade-offs between the different options and enough knowledge of the example boards to make a choice on which to explore further.

ELECTRONICS

Before we get stuck into the ins and outs of microcontroller and embedded computer boards, let's address some of the electronics components that you might want to connect to them.

Don't worry if you're scared of things such as having to learn soldering. You are unlikely to need it for your initial experiments. Most of the prototyping can be done on what are called *solderless breadboards*. They enable you to build components together into a circuit with just a push-fit connection, which also means you can experiment with different options quickly and easily.

When it comes to thinking about the electronics, it's useful to split them into two main categories:

Sensors: Sensors are the ways of getting information *into* your device, finding out things about your surroundings.

Actuators: Actuators are the *outputs* for the device—the motors, lights, and so on, which let your device do something to the outside world.

Within both categories, the electronic components can talk to the computer in a number of ways.

The simplest is through digital I/O, which has only two states: a button can either be pressed or not; or an LED can be on or off. These states are usually connected via general-purpose input/output (GPIO) pins and map a digital 0 in the processor to 0 volts in the circuit and the digital 1 to a set

voltage, usually the voltage that the processor is using to run (commonly 5V or 3.3V).

If you want a more nuanced connection than just on/off, you need an analogue signal. For example, if you wire up a potentiometer to let you read in the position of a rotary knob, you will get a varying voltage, depending on the knob's location. Similarly, if you want to run a motor at a speed other than off or full-speed, you need to feed it with a voltage somewhere between 0V and its maximum rating.

Because computers are purely digital devices, you need a way to translate between the analogue voltages in the real world and the digital of the computer.

An analogue-to-digital converter (ADC) lets you measure varying voltages. Microcontrollers often have a number of these converters built in. They will convert the voltage level between 0V and a predefined maximum (often the same 5V or 3.3V the processor is running at, but sometimes a fixed value such as 1V) into a number, depending on the accuracy of the ADC. The Arduino has 10-bit ADCs, which by default measure voltages between 0 and 5V. A voltage of 0 will give a reading of 0; a voltage of 5V would read 1023 (the maximum value that can be stored in a 10-bits); and voltages in between result in readings relative to the voltage. 1V would map to 205; a reading of 512 would mean the voltage was 2.5V; and so on.

The flipside of an ADC is a DAC, or digital-to-analogue converter. DACs let you generate varying voltages from a digital value but are less common as a standard feature of microcontrollers. This is due to a technique called *pulse-width modulation* (PWM), which gives an approximation to a DAC by rapidly turning a digital signal on and off so that the average value is the level you desire. PWM requires simpler circuitry, and for certain applica-tions, such as fading an LED, it is actually the preferred option.

For more complicated sensors and modules, there are interfaces such as Serial Peripheral Interface (SPI) bus and Inter-Integrated Circuit (I2C). These standardized mechanisms allow modules to communicate, so sensors or things such as Ethernet modules or SD cards can interface to the microcontroller.

Naturally, we cant cover all the possible sensors and actuators available, but we list some of the more common ones here to give a flavour of what is possible.

SENSORS
Pushbuttons and switches, which are probably the simplest sensors, allow some user input. Potentiometers (both rotary and linear) and rotary encoders enable you to measure movement.

Sensing the environment is another easy option. Light-dependent resistors (LDRs) allow measurement of ambient light levels, thermistors and other temperature sensors allow you to know how warm it is, and sensors to measure humidity or moisture levels are easy to build.

Microphones obviously let you monitor sounds and audio, but piezo elements (used in certain types of microphones) can also be used to respond to vibration.

Distance-sensing modules, which work by bouncing either an infrared or ultrasonic signal off objects, are readily available and as easy to interface to as a potentiometer.

ACTUATORS
One of the simplest and yet most useful actuators is light, because it is easy to create electronically and gives an obvious output. Light-emitting diodes (LEDs) typically come in red and green but also white and other colours.

RGB LEDs have a more complicated setup but allow you to mix the levels of red, green, and blue to make whatever colour of light you want. More complicated visual outputs also are available, such as LCD screens to display text or even simple graphics.

Piezo elements, as well as *responding* to vibration, can be used to *create* it, so you can use a piezo buzzer to create simple sounds and music. Alternatively, you can wire up outputs to speakers to create more complicated synthesized sounds.

Of course, for many tasks, you might also want to use components that *move* things in the real world. Solenoids can by used to create a single, sharp pushing motion, which could be useful for pushing a ball off a ledge or tapping a surface to make a musical sound.

More complicated again are motors. Stepper motors can be moved in *steps*, as the name implies. Usually, a fixed number of steps perform a full rotation. DC motors simply move at a given speed when told to. Both types of motor can be one-directional or move in both directions. Alternatively, if you want a motor that will turn to a given angle, you would need a servo. Although a servo is more controllable, it tends to have a shorter range of motion, often 180 or fewer degrees (whereas steppers and DC motors turn indefinitely). For all the kinds of motors that we've mentioned, you typically want to connect the motors to gears to alter the range of motion or convert circular movement to linear, and so on.

If you want to dig further into the ways of interfacing your computer or microcontroller with the real world, the "Interfacing with Hardware" page on the Arduino Playground website (http://playground.arduino.cc//Main/ InterfacingWithHardware) is a good place to start. Although Arduino-focused, most of the suggestions will translate to other platforms with minimal changes. For a more in-depth introduction to electronics, we recommend Electronics For Dummies *(Wiley, 2009).*

SCALING UP THE ELECTRONICS

From the perspective of the electronics, the starting point for prototyping is usually a "breadboard". This lets you push-fit components and wires to make up circuits without requiring any soldering and therefore makes experimen-tation easy. When you're happy with how things are wired up, it's common to solder the components onto some protoboard, which may be sufficient to make the circuit more permanent and prevent wires from going astray.

Moving beyond the protoboard option tends to involve learning how to lay out a PCB. This task isn't as difficult as it sounds, for simple circuits at least, and mainly involves learning how to use a new piece of software and understanding some new terminology.

For small production runs, you'll likely use through-hole components, so called because the legs of the component go through holes in the PCB and tend to be soldered by hand. You will often create your designs as companion boards to an existing microcontroller platform—generally called *shields* in the Arduino community. This approach lets you bootstrap production without worrying about designing the entire system from scratch.

Journey to a Circuit Board

Let's look at the evolution of part of the Bubblino circuitry, from initial testing, through prototype, to finished PCB:

The first step in creating your circuit is generally to build it up on a breadboard. This way, you can easily reconfigure things as you decide exactly how it should be laid out.

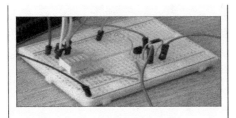

The breadboard.

When you are happy with how the circuit works, soldering it onto a stripboard will make the layout permanent. This means you can stop worrying about one of the wires coming loose, and if you're going to make only one copy of the circuit, that might be as far as you need take things.

When you want to scale things even further, moving to a combined board allows you to remove any unnecessary components from the microcon-troller board, and switching to surface mount components—where the legs of the chips are soldered onto the same surface as the chip—eases the board's assembly with automated manufacturing lines.

PCB design and the options for manufacturing are covered in much greater detail in Chapter 10, "Moving to Manufacture".

EMBEDDED COMPUTING BASICS

The rest of this chapter examines a number of different embedded comput-ing platforms, so it makes sense to first cover some of the concepts and terms that you will encounter along the way.

Providing background is especially important because many of you may have little or no idea about what a microcontroller is. Although we've been talking about computing power getting cheaper and more powerful, you cannot just throw a bunch of PC components into something and call it an Internet of Things product. If you've ever opened up a desktop PC, you've seen that it's a collection of discrete modules to provide different aspects of functionality. It has a main motherboard with its processor, one or two smaller circuit boards providing the RAM, and a hard disk to provide the long-term storage. So, it has a lot of components, which provide a variety of general-purpose functionality and which all take up a corresponding chunk of physical space.

MICROCONTROLLERS

Internet of Things devices take advantage of more tightly integrated and miniaturized solutions—from the most basic level of microcontrollers to more powerful system-on-chip (SoC) modules. These systems combine the processor, RAM, and storage onto a single chip, which means they are much more specialized, smaller than their PC equivalents, and also easier to build into a custom design.

These microcontrollers are the engines of countless sensors and automated factory machinery. They are the last bastions of 8-bit computing in a world that's long since moved to 32-bit and beyond. Microcontrollers are very limited in their capabilities—which is why 8-bit microcontrollers are still in use, although the price of 32-bit microcontrollers is now dropping to the level where they're starting to be edged out. Usually, they offer RAM capabilities measured in kilobytes and storage in the tens of kilobytes. However, they can still achieve a lot despite their limitations.

You'd be forgiven if the mention of 8-bit computing and RAM measured in kilobytes gives you flashbacks to the early home computers of the 1980s such as the Commodore 64 or the Sinclair ZX Spectrum. The 8-bit microcon-trollers have the same sort of internal workings and similar levels of memory to work with. There have been some improvements in the intervening years, though—the modern chips are much smaller, require less power, and run about five times faster than their 1980s counterparts.

Unlike the market for desktop computer processors, which is dominated by two manufacturers (Intel and AMD), the microcontroller market consists of many manufacturers. A better comparison is with the automotive market. In the same way that there are many different car manufacturers, each with a range of models for different uses, so there are lots of microcontroller manufacturers (Atmel, Microchip, NXP, Texas Instruments, to name a few), each with a range of chips for different applications.

The ubiquitous Arduino platform is based around Atmel's AVR ATmega family of microcontroller chips. The on-board inclusion of an assortment of GPIO pins and ADC circuitry means that microcontrollers are easy to wire up to all manner of sensors, lights, and motors. Because the devices using them are focused on performing one task, they can dispense with most of what we would term an operating system, resulting in a simpler and much slimmer code footprint than that of a SoC or PC solution.

In these systems, functions which require greater resource levels are usually provided by additional single-purpose chips which at times are more powerful than their controlling microcontroller. For example, the WizNet Ethernet chip used by the Arduino Ethernet has eight times more RAM than the Arduino itself.

SYSTEM-ON-CHIPS

In between the low-end microcontroller and a full-blown PC sits the SoC (for example, the BeagleBone or the Raspberry Pi). Like the microcontroller, these SoCs combine a processor and a number of peripherals onto a single chip but usually have more capabilities. The processors usually range from a few hundred megahertz, nudging into the gigahertz for top-end solutions, and include RAM measured in megabytes rather than kilobytes. Storage for SoC modules tends not to be included on the chip, with SD cards being a popular solution.

The greater capabilities of SoC mean that they need some sort of operating system to marshal their resources. A wide selection of embedded operating systems, both closed and open source, is available and from both specialised embedded providers and the big OS players, such as Microsoft and Linux.

Again, as the price falls for increased computing power, the popularity and familiarity of options such as Linux are driving its wider adoption.

CHOOSING YOUR PLATFORM

How to choose the *right* platform for your Internet of Things device is as easy a question to answer as working out the meaning of life. This isn't to say that it's an impossible question—more that there are almost as many answers as there are possible devices. The platform you choose depends on the particular blend of price, performance, and capabilities that suit what you're trying to achieve. And just because you settle on one solution, that doesn't mean somebody else wouldn't have chosen a completely different set of options to solve the same problem.

Start by choosing a platform to prototype in. The following sections discuss some of the factors that you need to weigh—and possibly play off against each other—when deciding how to build your device.

Processor Speed

The processor speed, or clock speed, of your processor tells you how fast it can process the individual instructions in the machine code for the program it's running. Naturally, a faster processor speed means that it can execute instructions more quickly.

The clock speed is still the simplest proxy for raw computing power, but it isn't the only one. You might also make a comparison based on millions of instructions per second (MIPS), depending on what numbers are being reported in the datasheet or specification for the platforms you are comparing.

Some processors may lack hardware support for floating-point calculations, so if the code involves a lot of complicated mathematics, a by-the-numbers slower processor with hardware floating-point support could be faster than a slightly higher performance processor without it.

Generally, you will use the processor speed as one of a number of factors when weighing up similar systems. Microcontrollers tend to be clocked at speeds in the tens of MHz, whereas SoCs run at hundreds of MHz or possibly low GHz.

If your project doesn't require heavyweight processing—for example, if it needs only networking and fairly basic sensing—then some sort of micro-controller will be fast enough. If your device will be crunching lots of data—for example, processing video in real time—then you'll be looking at a SoC platform.

RAM

RAM provides the working memory for the system. If you have more RAM, you may be able to do more things or have more flexibility over your choice of coding algorithm. If you're handling large datasets on the device, that could govern how much space you need. You can often find ways to work around memory limitations, either in code (see Chapter 8, "Techniques for Writing Embedded Code") or by handing off processing to an online service (see Chapter 7, "Prototyping Online Components").

It is difficult to give exact guidelines to the amount of RAM you will need, as it will vary from project to project. However, microcontrollers with less than 1KB of RAM are unlikely to be of interest, and if you want to run standard encryption protocols, you will need at least 4KB, and preferably more.

For SoC boards, particularly if you plan to run Linux as the operating system, we recommend at least 256MB.

Networking

How your device connects to the rest of the world is a key consideration for Internet of Things products. Wired Ethernet is often the simplest for the user—generally plug and play—and cheapest, but it requires a physical cable. Wireless solutions obviously avoid that requirement but introduce a more complicated configuration.

WiFi is the most widely deployed to provide an existing infrastructure for connections, but it can be more expensive and less optimized for power consumption than some of its competitors.

Other short-range wireless can offer better power-consumption profiles or costs than WiFi but usually with the trade-off of lower bandwidth. ZigBee is one such technology, aimed particularly at sensor networks and scenarios such as home automation. The recent Bluetooth LE protocol (also known as Bluetooth 4.0) has a very low power-consumption profile similar to ZigBee's and could see more rapid adoption due to its inclusion into standard Bluetooth chips included in phones and laptops. There is, of course, the existing Bluetooth standard as another possible choice. And at the boring-but-very-cheap end of the market sit long-established options such as RFM12B which operate in the 434 MHz radio spectrum, rather than the 2.4 GHz range of the other options we've discussed.

For remote or outdoor deployment, little beats simply using the mobile phone networks. For low-bandwidth, higher-latency communication, you could use something as basic as SMS; for higher data rates, you will use the same data connections, like 3G, as a smartphone.

USB

If your device can rely on a more powerful computer being nearby, tethering to it via USB can be an easy way to provide both power and networking. You can buy some of the microcontrollers in versions which include support for USB, so choosing one of them reduces the need for an extra chip in your circuit.

Instead of the microcontroller presenting itself as a device, some can also act as the USB "host". This configuration lets you connect items that would normally expect to be connected to a computer—devices such as phones, for example, using the Android ADK, additional storage capacity, or WiFi dongles.

Devices such as WiFi dongles often depend on additional software on the host system, such as networking stacks, and so are better suited to the more computer-like option of SoC.

Power Consumption

Faster processors are often more power hungry than slower ones. For devices which might be portable or rely on an unconventional power supply (batteries, solar power) depending on where they are installed, power consumption may be an issue. Even with access to mains electricity, the power consumption may be something to consider because lower consumption may be a desirable feature.

However, processors may have a minimal power-consumption sleep mode. This mode may allow you to use a faster processor to quickly perform operations and then return to low-power sleep. Therefore, a more powerful processor may *not* be a disadvantage even in a low-power embedded device.

Interfacing with Sensors and Other Circuitry

In addition to talking to the Internet, your device needs to interact with something else—either sensors to gather data about its environment; or motors, LEDs, screens, and so on, to provide output. You could connect to the circuitry through some sort of peripheral bus—SPI and I2C being common ones—or through ADC or DAC modules to read or write varying voltages; or through generic GPIO pins, which provide digital on/off inputs or outputs. Different microcontrollers or SoC solutions offer different mixtures of these interfaces in differing numbers.

Physical Size and Form Factor

The continual improvement in manufacturing techniques for silicon chips means that we've long passed the point where the limiting factor in the size of a chip is the amount of space required for all the transistors and other components that make up the circuitry on the silicon. Nowadays, the size is governed by the number of connections it needs to make to the surrounding components on the PCB. With the traditional through -hole design, most commonly used for home-made circuits, the legs of the chip are usually spaced at 0.1" intervals. Even if your chip has relatively few connections to the surrounding circuit—16 pins is nothing for such a chip—you will end up with over 1.5" (~4cm) for the perimeter of your chip. More complex chips can easily run to over a hundred connections; finding room for a chip with a 10" (25cm) perimeter might be a bit tricky!

You can pack the legs closer together with surface-mount technology because it doesn't require holes to be drilled in the board for connections. Combining that with the trick of hiding some of the connections on the underside of the chip means that it is possible to use the complex designs without resorting to PCBs the size of a table.

The limit to the size that each connection can be reduced to is then governed by the capabilities and tolerances of your manufacturing process. Some surface-mount designs are big enough for home-etched PCBs and can be hand-soldered. Others require professionally produced PCBs and accurate pick-and-place machines to locate them correctly.

Due to these trade-offs in size versus manufacturing complexity, many chip designs are available in a number of different form factors, known as *packages*. This lets the circuit designer choose the form that best suits his particular application.

All three chips pictured in the following figure provide identical functional-ity because they are all AVR ATmega328 microcontrollers. The one on the left is the through-hole package, mounted here in a socket so that it can be swapped out without soldering. The two others are surface mount, in two different packages, showing the reduction in size but at the expense of ease of soldering.

Through-hole versus surface-mount ATmega328 chips.

Looking at the ATmega328 leads us nicely into comparing some specific embedded computing platforms. We can start with a look at one which so popularized the ATmega328 that a couple of years ago it led to a worldwide shortage of the chip in the through-hole package, as for a short period demand outstripped supply.

Chapter 5.
IoT & Cities

Cities around the world have been the locus of innovation in the use of the Internet of Things. Through "smart city" initiatives and entrepreneurship, cities are experimenting with IoT applications to improve services, relieve traffic congestion, conserve water and energy, and improve quality of life. Large, concentrated populations and complex infrastructure make cities a target-rich environment for IoT applications. And cities have the most to gain: they are engines of global economic growth, and with urbanization in developing economies, 60 percent of the world's population—about 4.7 billion people—will live in cities in 2025.

We found the highest economic impact of IoT applications we analyzed to be concentrated in a few use areas, such as public health and safety, transportation, and resource management. IoT applications in public safety and health include air and water quality monitoring. Transportation applications range from traffic-control systems to smart parking meters to autonomous vehicles. Resource and infrastructure management uses include sensors and smart meters to better manage water and electric infrastructure.

Based on current adoption and likely growth rates, we estimate that the economic impact of the Internet of Things in cities (for the applications we size) could be $930 billion to $1.7 trillion globally in 2025. Our estimates of potential impact are based on the value of improved health and safety (automobile deaths avoided and reduction in pollution-related illnesses, for example), the value of time saved through IoT applications, and more efficient use of resources. We estimate the economic impact of illness and deaths avoided by IoT applications using quality-adjusted life years, a measure of the economic value of a year of perfect health in a particular economy. There are many additional social and environmental benefits, such as tracking lost children and higher social engagement, which we do not attempt to size.

Reaching this level of impact depends on addressing the technical and regulatory issues common to other settings—the need for lower-cost hardware and building protections for privacy and security. In cities, there also will need to be political consensus to support IoT applications, which in many cases will require investment of public funds. For example, the decision to install adaptive traffic-control systems that adjust traffic lights using sensor data will require motivated city authorities and politicians.

Definition

We define the city setting to include all urban settlements, consistent with the definition used by the United Nations in its World Urbanization Prospects report. In our estimates of IoT impact in cities, we do not include applications used in homes or the use of IoT devices for health and fitness, which are counted in the home and human settings.

Exhibit 24 illustrates some of the emerging applications of IoT technology that can improve the performance of resource management, transportation, and public safety and health.

Potential for economic impact

For the applications we sized, we estimate that the potential economic impact of the Internet of Things in the city setting could exceed $1.7 trillion per year in 2025. The single most economically important application could be public health, where we estimate that nearly $700 billion a year of value might be captured in 2025 from the improved health outcomes that would result from water and air monitoring. Taken together, however, transportation applications could have even larger economic impact—more than $800 billion per year in 2025. Traffic applications, including real-time traffic flow management, smart meters and more efficient use of public transportation (reducing wait times by using real-time bus and train information), could be worth more than $570 billion a year globally. Autonomous vehicles could contribute as much as $235 billion by reducing traffic accidents, fuel consumption, and carbon emissions.

Public health and safety

IoT technology has several applications in urban public health and safety, which could have an economic impact of about $700 billion per year in 2015. These applications include using video cameras for crime monitoring, improving emergency services and disaster response, and monitoring street lights and the structural health of buildings. The biggest impact, however, would come from the application of IoT technology in air and water quality monitoring.

Air and water quality monitoring

The World Health Organization estimates that 3.7 million deaths were linked to outdoor air pollution in 2012, with the bulk of deaths occurring in low- and middle-income countries. IoT technology provides cities and citizens with the means to gather real-time data on air and water quality from thousands of location and to pinpoint problems at the neighborhood or even housing unit level. Efforts such as Air Quality Egg to crowdsource air quality readings and the Floating Sensor Network program at the University of California at Berkeley are showing how low-cost, communicating sensors can be used to gather much more detailed data on what residents are breathing and drinking. Similar approaches can be used to monitor water supply at the tap. Greater awareness and accountability will improve air and water quality. For example, if monitoring leads to effective pollution-reduction strategies, cities could cut particulate matter pollution from 70 micrograms per cubic meter to 20 micrograms per cubic meter. We estimate that this could cut deaths related to air pollution by around 15 percent.

Crime detection and monitoring

Many cities already have security cameras and some have gunshot recognition sensors. IoT will enable these cameras and sensors to automatically detect unusual activities, such as someone leaving a bag unattended, and to trigger a rapid response. Such solutions are already in use in Glasgow, Scotland, and in Memphis, Tennessee, in the United States. Cities that have implemented such systems claim a 10 to 30 percent decrease in crime. We estimate the economic impact of crime reduction on this scale could be more than $30 billion per year.

Transportation

In total, improvements in transportation—measured mostly in time saved by travelers—could have an economic impact of $443 billion to $808 billion per year in 2025.

Centralized and adaptive traffic management

Adaptive traffic control uses real-time data to adjust the timing of traffic lights to improve traffic flow. A centralized control system collects data from sensors installed at intersections to monitor traffic flow. Based on volume, the system adjusts the length of red and green lights to ensure smooth flow. Abu Dhabi recently implemented such a system, which covers 125 main intersections in the city. The system also can give priority to buses, ambulances, or emergency vehicles. For example, if a bus is five minutes behind schedule, traffic signals at the intersection are adjusted to prioritize passage for the bus. Use of adaptive traffic control has been shown to speed traffic flow by between 5 and 25 percent. We estimate that adaptive traffic control and smart meters could reduce time spent in traffic jams and looking for parking spaces by 10 to 15 percent, which could be worth more than $500 billion per year globally in 2025. There could be additional benefits, such as reduced CO_2 emissions and postponing or avoiding investment in new roads.

Autonomous vehicles

The use of autonomous vehicles in urban areas can create economic value in a number of ways—freeing up time for drivers; reducing traffic accidents, injuries, and fatalities; saving fuel and raising average highway speeds; and expanding the capacity of parking facilities through self-parking. Autonomous vehicles are already in use in industrial environments such as mines (see worksite setting above). The self-driving passenger car has been in development for several years, and some manufacturers are already offering IoT-based features in production models such as automatic braking for collision avoidance. Some carmakers expect to have self-driving cars on the road by 2020, pending regulatory approval—a non-trivial hurdle. Still, we expect that fully autonomous cars (which require no driver intervention) and partially autonomous cars (which could take over control of all safety-critical functions under certain conditions) to be a reality in cities around the world in 2025. We assume that in 2025, between 1 and 2 percent of light vehicles on the road—

15 million to 30 million vehicles—could be fully self-driving.50 We assume that the penetration of semi-autonomous vehicles could be 12 to 15 percent.

The economic impact of autonomous vehicles in urban settings could be $204 billion to $235 billion per year in 2025. The economic benefit is calculated based on the value of time and fuel saved, traffic fatalities avoided, and greater utilization of assets such as parking spaces. Globally, 1.2 billion people spend 50 minutes on average driving in cars each day. Autonomous vehicles offer the potential to improve traffic flow and free up time spent in the car for other activities. We estimate that time saved through adoption of autonomous vehicles could be worth $15 billion to $25 billion in cities.

In addition, autonomous and partially autonomous vehicles could drastically reduce car accidents. More than 90 percent of US car crashes can be attributed to human error, and more than 40 percent of traffic fatalities involve driver impairment due to alcohol, distraction, drugs, or fatigue. We estimate that traffic accidents could be reduced by 90 percent with the adoption of fully autonomous vehicles and by 40 percent with partially autonomous vehicles, saving 95,000 lives per year, for an estimated economic impact of $180 billion to $200 billion per year.

Autonomous vehicles also can reduce fuel consumption by driving more efficiently. Under computer control, autonomous vehicles would not indulge in wasteful driving behaviors, and with vehicle-to-vehicle communications, cars can travel close together at highway speeds, reducing wind resistance and raising average speed. Autonomous driving could also enable radical changes in automobile design that would make cars lighter and more fuel-efficient. We estimate that fuel consumption could be as much as 15 percent lower.

Finally, because fully autonomous vehicles can park themselves, there is no need to use space between cars in a parking lot or deck to accommodate door openings. This could free up 15 percent of parking space. In addition, autonomous vehicles that drive themselves to parking areas could reduce the need for parking lots and garages in city centers—cars could drop off passengers at their workplaces and even pick up passengers leaving the city center as they proceed to remote parking areas. Adoption of self-driving cars could also lead to new car-pooling and ride-sharing options, which would reduce overall, demand for parking.

Bus and train schedule management

There is a substantial opportunity to save time for riders of public transit by using IoT data. With sensors capturing real-time location data of trains and buses, commuters can shrink the "reliability buffer"—the extra time a traveler builds into a trip to account for possible delays. The buffer can be as much as 70 percent of total trip time.51 Using an app (on a computer or smartphone), commuters can time their exits from home or office (or anywhere in the city) to arrive at the station or bus stop just in time for their trips. In our calculations, we assume that in advanced economies, the average wait time per trip for commuters is 12 minutes; in developing economies, we assume 21 minutes.

We further estimate that real-time data could allow commuters to reduce waiting time by approximately 15 percent. Also, given the widespread use of existing GPS-enabled monitoring systems, we assume that development and use of transit-tracking apps will be rapid. Real-time information for buses and trains is already available in New York City, Chicago, Singapore, and some other major cities and is spreading quickly.

We calculate the value of wait time eliminated by looking at the average wage rates in advanced and developing economies and applying a 70 percent discount, which analysts typically use to value non-work time. We arrived at an estimate of $13 billion to $63 billion per year from the potential impact of using IoT to manage bus and train commuting. This does not include other potential gains by transit operators from using IoT data to adjust schedules and routes (reducing service at certain hours or skipping underutilized stops, for example).

There could be additional benefits, such as reduced CO_2 emissions and postponing or avoiding investment in new roads.

Resource/infrastructure management

IoT technology has already demonstrated its potential for monitoring and managing critical urban resources, such as water, sewage, and electric systems. Using sensors to monitor performance across their networks, operators of power and water systems can detect flaws such as leaks in water mains or overheating transformers, enabling operators to prevent costly failures and reduce losses. We estimate that these applications could have an impact of $33 billion to $64 billion per year globally in 2025. Smart meters, which are already being implemented in numerous cities, not only allow utility companies to automate meter reading, but also can enable demand-management programs (encouraging energy conservation through variable pricing, for example), and detect theft of service. By 2025, we estimate that 80 percent of utilities in advanced-economy cities and 50 percent of utilities in developing-economy cities will have adopted smart meters, creating potential value of $14 billion to $25 billion in 2025. Use of IoT technology in distribution and substation automation could have an additional impact of $13 billion to $24 billion per year in 2025. In water systems, we estimate that IoT technology (smart meters) could provide value of $7 billion to $14 billion per year.

Human productivity

The primary ways in which IoT technology would be used to increase productivity of individual workers in urban environments would be through monitoring mobile workers such as motor vehicle operators, building cleaners, pest control workers, and sales representatives. The increased productivity of such workers and IoT-enabled processes to raise productivity of technical and knowledge workers in cities could be worth $2.7 billion to $6.0 billion per year globally in 2025. This assumes an estimated 5 percent increase in productivity of mobile workers and a 3 to 4 percent increase in productivity of knowledge workers.

Enablers and barriers

Multiple factors would need to come together for the Internet of Things to achieve its maximum potential in cities. We expect adoption rates for the IoT applications we size could reach 40 to 80 percent in cities In advanced economies in 2025, and 20 to 40 percent in cities in developing economies. This disparity is a function of having both the ability to fund IoT improvements, which often require public investment, and access to the skills needed for successful implementation and operation of IoT-based systems. The ability to fund IoT investments depends upon the wealth of the city and the government's ability to access investment vehicles or use tax revenue. Another factor is a responsive citizenry. In cities with a high proportion of well-educated residents, demand will likely be higher for the benefits that IoT applications can bring. This can create a virtuous cycle: as successful applications build awareness of benefits, more citizens would demand them.

Achieving maximum potential benefit from IoT in cities also requires interoperability among IoT systems. If autonomous vehicles, a centralized traffic-control system, and smart parking meters were all on speaking terms (so to speak), the commuter's autonomous car could communicate with the centralized traffic system to select the best route, then guide the commuter to the most convenient meter space or the cheapest parking facility where a fully autonomous vehicle could park itself. Interoperability would vastly increase the value of IoT applications in urban settings and encourage many more cities to adopt them.

Cities must also have the technical capacity in their agencies and departments, and committed leadership is essential. To deploy and manage IoT applications requires technical depth that most city governments currently do not possess. Cities that develop this capacity will be ahead in the race to capture IoT benefits. City leaders must also have the political will to drive IoT adoption—to find the funding and make the organizational changes needed to regulate or operate the systems that use IoT technology.

Last but not least, IoT will be broadly adopted only if city governments and the public are assured of the security of IoT-enabled systems. The potential risks are not to be underestimated: malicious parties that find ways to interfere with traffic-control systems or the programs that guide autonomous vehicles could cause enormous damage. Technology vendors will not only need to provide secure systems, but they will also have to convince city governments and residents that the systems truly are secure.

Chapter 6.
IoT Using ARDUINO

Without a doubt, the poster child for the Internet of Things, and physical computing in general, is the Arduino.

These days the Arduino project covers a number of microcontroller boards, but its birth was in Ivrea in Northern Italy in 2005. A group from the Interaction Design Institute Ivrea (IDII) wanted a board for its design students to use to build interactive projects. An assortment of boards was around at that time, but they tended to be expensive, hard to use, or both.

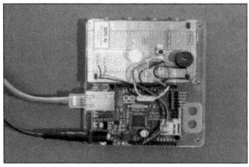

An Arduino Ethernet board, plugged in, wired up to a circuit and ready for use.

So, the team put together a board which was cheap to buy—around £20— and included an onboard serial connection to allow it to be easily pro-grammed. Combined with an extension of the Wiring software environment, it made a huge impact on the world of physical computing.

Wiring: Sketching in Hardware

Another child of the IDII is the Wiring project. In the summer of 2003, Hernando Barragán started a project to make it easier to experiment with electronics and hardware. As the project website (http://wiring.org.co/about. html) puts it:

"The idea is to write a few lines of code, connect a few electronic components to the hardware of choice and observe how a light turns on when person approaches to it, write a few more lines add another sensor and see how this light changes when the illumination level in a room decreases.

This process is called sketching with hardware—a way to explore lots of ideas very quickly, by selecting the more interesting ones, refining them, and producing prototypes in an iterative process."

The Wiring platform provides an abstraction layer over the hardware, so the users need not worry about the exact way to, say, turn on a GPIO pin, and can focus on the problem they're trying to explore or solve.

That abstraction also enables the platform to run on a variety of hardware boards. There have been a number of Wiring boards since the project started, although they have been eclipsed by the runaway success of the project that took the Wiring platform and targeted a lower-end and cheaper AVR processor: the Arduino project.

A decision early on to make the code and schematics open source meant that the Arduino board could outlive the demise of the IDII and flourish. It also meant that people could adapt and extend the platform to suit their own needs.

As a result, an entire ecosystem of boards, add-ons, and related kits has flourished. The Arduino team's focus on simplicity rather than raw perfor-mance for the code has made the Arduino the board of choice in almost every beginner's physical computing project, and the open source ethos has encouraged the community to share circuit diagrams, parts lists, and source code. It's almost the case that whatever your project idea is, a quick search on Google for it, in combination with the word "Arduino", will throw up at least one project that can help bootstrap what you're trying to achieve. If you prefer learning from a book, we recommend picking up a copy of *Arduino For Dummies*, by John Nussey (Wiley, 2013).

The "standard" Arduino board has gone through a number of iterations: Arduino NG, Diecimila, Duemilanove, and Uno.

The Uno features an ATmega328 microcontroller and a USB socket for connection to a computer. It has 32KB of storage and 2KB of RAM, but don't let those meagre amounts of memory put you off; you can achieve a surprising amount despite the limitations.

The Uno also provides 14 GPIO pins (of which 6 can also provide PWM output) and 6 10 -bit resolution ADC pins. The ATmega's serial port is made available through both the IO pins, and, via an additional chip, the USB connector.

If you need more space or a greater number of inputs or outputs, look at the Arduino Mega 2560. It marries a more powerful ATmega microcontroller to the same software environment, providing 256KB of Flash storage, 8KB of RAM, three more serial ports, a massive 54 GPIO pins (14 of those also capable of PWM) and 16 ADCs. Alternatively, the more recent Arduino Due has a 32-bit ARM core microcontroller and is the first of the Arduino boards to use this architecture. Its specs are similar to the Mega's, although it ups the RAM to 96KB.

DEVELOPING ON THE ARDUINO

More than just specs, the experience of working with a board may be the most important factor, at least at the prototyping stage. As previously mentioned, the Arduino is optimized for simplicity, and this is evident from the way it is packaged for use. Using a single USB cable, you can not only

The Arduino doesn't, by default, run an OS as such, only the bootloader, which simplifies the code-pushing process described previously. When you switch on the board, it simply runs the code that you have compiled until the board is switched off again (or the code crashes).

It is, however, possible to upload an OS to the Arduino, usually a lightweight real-time operating system (RTOS) such as FreeRTOS/DuinOS. The main advantage of one of these operating systems is their built-in support for multitasking. However, for many purposes, you can achieve reasonable results with a simpler task-dispatching library.

If you dislike the simple life, it is even possible to compile code without using the IDE but by using the toolset for the Arduino's chip—for example, for all the boards until the recent ARM-based Due, the avr-gcc toolset.

The avr-gcc toolset (www.nongnu.org/avr-libc/) is the collection of programs that let you compile code to run on the AVR chips used by the rest of the Arduino boards and flash the resultant executable to the chip. It is used by the Arduino IDE behind the scenes but can be used directly, as well.

Language

The language usually used for Arduino is a slightly modified dialect of C++ derived from the Wiring platform. It includes some libraries used to read and write data from the I/O pins provided on the Arduino and to do some basic handling for "interrupts" (a way of doing multitasking, at a very low level). This variant of C++ tries to be forgiving about the ordering of code; for example, it allows you to call functions before they are defined. This alteration is just a nicety, but it is useful to be able to order things in a way that the code is easy to read and maintain, given that it tends to be written in a single file.
The code needs to provide only two routines:

setup(): This routine is run once when the board first boots. You could use it to set the modes of I/O pins to input or output or to prepare a data structure which will be used throughout the program.

loop(): This routine is run repeatedly in a tight loop while the Arduino is switched on. Typically, you might check some input, do some calculation on it, and perhaps do some output in response.

To avoid getting into the details of programming languages in this chapter, we just compare a simple example across all the boards—blinking a single LED:

Pin 13 has an LED connected on most Arduino boards.

give it a name:

```
int led = 13;
// the setup routine runs once when you press reset: void setup() {

// initialize the  digital pin as an output.
pinMode(led,
OUTPUT);
}
//   the    loopruns over and over again
routine        forever:
void loop() {
              HIGH)
digitalWrite(led,;      // turn the LED on
delay(1000);           // wait for a second
digitalWrite(led, LOW); // turn the LED off
delay(1000);           // wait for a second
}
```

Reading through this code, you'll see that the setup() function does very little; it just sets up that pin number 13 is the one we're going to control (because it is wired up to an LED).

Then, in loop(), the LED is turned on and then off, with a delay of a second between each flick of the (electronic) switch. With the way that the Arduino environment works, whenever it reaches the end of one cycle—on; wait a second; off; wait a second—and drops out of the loop() function, it simply calls loop() again to repeat the process.

Debugging

Because C++ is a compiled language, a fair number of errors, such as bad syntax or failure to declare variables, are caught at compilation time. Because this happens on your computer, you have ample opportunity to get detailed and possibly helpful information from the compiler about what the problem is.
Although you need some debugging experience to be able to identify certain compiler errors, others, like this one, are relatively easy to understand:

Blink.cpp: In function 'void loop()':Blink:21: error:'digitalWritee' was not declared in this scope

When the code is pushed to the Arduino, the rules of the game change, however. Because the Arduino isn't generally connected to a screen, it is hard for it to tell you when something goes wrong. Even if the code compiled successfully, certain errors still happen. An error could be raised that can't be handled, such as a division by zero, or trying to access the tenth element of a 9-element list. Or perhaps your program leaks memory and eventually just stops working. Or (and worse) a programming error might make the code continue to work dutifully but give entirely the wrong results.

If Bubblino stops blowing bubbles, how can we distinguish between the following cases?

Nobody has mentioned us on Twitter.

The Twitter search API has stopped working. Bubblino can't connect to the Internet.
Bubblino has crashed due to a programming error.

Bubblino is working, but the motor of the bubble machine has failed. Bubblino is powered off.

Adrian likes to joke that he can debug many problems by looking at the flashing lights at Bubblino's Ethernet port, which flashes while Bubblino connects to DNS and again when it connects to Twitter's search API, and so on. (He also jokes that we can discount the "programming error" option and that the main reason the motor would fail is that Hakim has poured bubble mix into the wrong hole. Again.) But while this approach might help distinguish two of the preceding cases, it doesn't help with the others and isn't useful if you are releasing the product into a mass market!
The first commercially available version of the WhereDial has a bank of half a dozen LEDs specifically for consumer-level debugging. In the case of an error, the pattern of lights showing may help customers fix their problem or help flesh out details for a support request.

Runtime programming errors may be tricky to trap because although the C++ language has exception handling, the avr-gcc compiler doesn't support it (probably due to the relatively high memory "cost" of handling exceptions); so the Arduino platform doesn't let you use the usual try...

catch... logic.

Effectively, this means that you need to check your data before using it: if a number might conceivably be zero, check that before trying to divide by it. Test that your indexes are within bounds. To avoid memory leaks, look at the tips on writing code for embedded devices in Chapter 8, "Techniques for Writing Embedded Code".

Rear view of a transparent WhereDial. The bank of LEDs can be seen in the middle of the green board, next to the red "error" LED.

But code isn't, in general, created perfect: in the meantime you need ways to identify where the errors are occurring so that you can bullet-proof them for next time. In the absence of a screen, the Arduino allows you to write information over the USB cable using Serial.write(). Although you can use the facility to communicate all kinds of data, debugging information can be particularly useful. The Arduino IDE provides a serial monitor which echoes the data that the Arduino has sent over the USB cable. This could include any textual information, such as logging information, comments, and details about the data that the Arduino is receiving and processing (to double-check that your calculations are doing the right thing).

SOME NOTES ON THE HARDWARE
The Arduino exposes a number of GPIO pins and is usually supplied with "headers" (plastic strips that sit on the pin holes, that provide a convenient solderless connection for wires, especially with a "jumper" connection). The headers are optimised for prototyping and for being able to change the purpose of the Arduino easily.

Each pin is clearly labelled on the controller board. The details of pins vary from the smaller boards such as the Nano, the classic form factor of the Uno, and the larger boards such as the Mega or the Due. In general, you have power outputs such as 5 volts or 3.3 volts (usually labelled 5V and 3V3, or perhaps just 3V), one or more electric ground connections (GND), num-bered digital pins, and numbered analogue pins prefixed with an *A*.

Close-up of an Arduino Leonardo board. Note the labeling of the power and analogue input connections.

You can power the Arduino using a USB connection from your computer. This capability is usually quite convenient during prototyping because you need the serial connection in any case to program the board. The Arduino also has a socket for an external power supply, which you might be more likely to use if you distribute the project. Either way should be capable of powering the microcontroller and the usual electronics that you might attach to it. (In the case of larger items, such as motors, you may have to attach external power and make that available selectively to the component using transistors.)

Outside of the standard boards, a number of them are focused on a particu-lar niche application—for example, the Arduino Ethernet has an on-board Ethernet chip and trades the USB socket for an Ethernet one, making it easier to hook up to the Internet.

This is obviously a strong contender for a useful board for Internet of Things projects.

The LilyPad has an entirely different specialism, as it has a flattened form (shaped, as the name suggests, like a flower with the I/O capabilities exposed on its "petals") and is designed to make it easy to wire up with conductive thread, and so a boon for wearable technology projects.

Choosing one of the specialist boards isn't the only way to extend the capabilities of your Arduino. Most of the boards share the same layout of the assorted GPIO, ADC, and power pins, and you are able to piggyback an additional circuit board on top of the Arduino which can contain all manner of componentry to give the Arduino extra capabilities.

In the Arduino world, these add-on boards are called *shields*, perhaps because they cover the actual board as if protecting it.

Some shields provide networking capabilities—Ethernet, WiFi, or Zigbee wireless, for example. Motor shields make it simple to connect motors and servos; there are shields to hook up mobile phone LCD screens; others to provide capacitive sensing; others to play MP3 files or WAV files from an SD card; and all manner of other possibilities—so much so that an entire website, http://shieldlist.org/, is dedicated to comparing and documenting them.

In terms of functionality, a standard Arduino with an Ethernet shield is equivalent to an Arduino Ethernet. However, the latter is thinner (because it has all the components laid out on a single board) but loses the convenient USB connection. (You can still connect to it to push code or communicate over the serial connection by using a supplied adaptor.)

OPENNESS

The Arduino project is completely open hardware and an open hardware success story.

The only part of the project protected is the Arduino trademark, so they can control the quality of any boards calling themselves an Arduino. In addition to the code being available to download freely, the circuit board schematics and even the EAGLE PCB design files are easily found on the Arduino website.

This culture of sharing has borne fruit in many derivative boards being produced by all manner of people. Some are merely minor variations on the main Arduino Uno, but many others introduce new features or form factors that the core Arduino team have overlooked.
In some cases, such as with the wireless-focused Arduino Fio board, what starts as a third-party board (it was originally the Funnel IO) is later adopted as an official Arduino-approved board.

Arduino Case Study: The Good Night Lamp

While at the IDII, Alexandra Deschamps-Sonsino came up with the idea of an Internet-connected table or bedside lamp. A simple, consumer device, this lamp would be paired with another lamp anywhere in the world, allowing it to switch the other lamp on and off, and vice versa. Because light is integrated into our daily routine, seeing when our loved ones turn, for example, their bedside lamp on or off gives us a calm and ambient view onto their lives.

This concept was ahead of its time in 2005, but the project has now been spun into its own company, the Good Night Lamp. The product consists of a "big lamp" which is paired with one or more "little lamps". The big lamp has its own switch and is designed to be used like a normal lamp. The little lamps, however, don't have switches but instead reflect the state of the big lamp.

Adrian was involved since the early stages as Chief Technology Officer. Adrian and the rest of the team's familiarity with Arduino led to it being an obvious choice as the prototyping platform. In addition, as the lamps are designed to be a consumer product rather than a technical product, and are targeted at a mass market, design, cost, and ease of use are also important. The Arduino platform is simple enough that it is possible to reduce costs and size substantially by choosing which components you need in the production version.

A key challenge in creating a mass-market connected device is finding a convenient way for consumers, some of whom are non-technical, to connect the device to the Internet. Even if the user has WiFi installed, entering authentication details for your home network on a device that has no keyboard or screen presents challenges. As well as looking into options for the best solution for this issue, the Good Night Lamp team are also building a version which connects over the mobile phone networks via GSM or 3G. This option fits in with the team's vision of connecting people via a "physical social network", even if they are not otherwise connected to the Internet.

Arduino Case Study: BakerTweet

The BakerTweet device (www.bakertweet.com/) is effectively a physical client for Twitter designed for use in a bakery. A baker may want to let customers know that a certain product has just come out of the ovens—fresh bread, hot muffins, cupcakes laden with icing—yet the environment he would want to tweet from contains hot ovens, flour dust, and sticky dough and batter, all of which would play havoc with the electronics, keyboard, and screen of a computer, tablet, or phone. Staff of design agency Poke in London wanted to know when their local bakery had just produced a fresh batch of their favourite bread and cake, so they designed a proof of concept to make it possible.

Because BakerTweet communicates using WiFi, bakeries, typically not built to accommodate Ethernet cables, can install it. BakerTweet exposes the functional-ity of

Twitter in a "bakery-proof" box with more robust electronics than a general-purpose computer, and a simplified interface that can be used by fingers covered in flour and dough. It was designed with an Arduino, an Ethernet Shield, and a WiFi adapter. As well as the Arduino simply controlling a third-party service (Twitter), it is also hooked up to a custom service which allows the baker to configure the messages to be sent.

Arduino: Getting Started

Arduino is an open-source electronics platform based on easy-to-use hardware and software. Arduino boards are able to read inputs – light on a sensor, a finger on a button, or a Twitter message – and turn it into an output – activating a motor, turning on an LED, publishing something online. You can tell your board what to do by sending a set of instructions to the microcontroller on the board. To do so you use the Arduino programming language (based on Wiring), and the Arduino Software (IDE), based on Processing.

1. Prepare Tools and Parts you'll need to make sure you have the following items.
- Arduino Uno Board
- Breadboard – half size
- Jumper Wires
- USB Cable
- LED (5mm)
- Push button switch
- 10k Ohm Resistor
- 220 Ohm Resistor

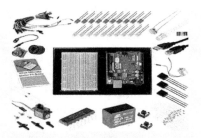

2. Download The Software

The Arduino IDE is the interface where we will write the sketches that tell the board what to do.

Download the the latest version of this software on the Arduino, corresponds to your Operating System on desktop.

3. Familiar with IDEOnce the software has been installed on your computer, go ahead and open it up. This is the Arduino IDE and is the place where all the programming will happen.

Menu Bar: Gives you access to the tools needed for creating and saving Arduino sketches.

Verify Button: Compiles your code and checks for errors in spelling or syntax.

Upload Button: Sends the code to the board that's connected such as Arduino Uno in this case. Lights on the board will blink rapidly when uploading.

New Sketch: Opens up a new window containing a blank sketch.

Sketch Name: When the sketch is saved, the name of the sketch is displayed here.

Open Existing Sketch: Allows you to open a saved sketch or one from the stored examples.

Save Sketch: This saves the sketch you currently have open.Serial Monitor: When the board is connected, this will display the serial information of your

ArduinoCode Area: This area is where you compose the code of the sketch that tells the board what to do.

Message Area: This area tells you the status on saving, code compiling, errors and more.

Text Console: Shows the details of an error messages, size of the program that was compiled and additional info.

Board and Serial Port: Tells you what board is being used and what serial port it's connected to.

4. Connect Your Arduino Uno

At this point you are ready to connect your Arduino to your computer. Plug one end of the USB cable to the Arduino Uno and then the other end of the USB to your computer's USB port.Once the board is connected, you will need to go to Tools then Board then finally select Arduino Uno.

Now, you have to tell the Arduino which port you are using on your computer.To select the port, go to Tools then Port then select the port that says Arduino.

Now, the system to develop the project is ready.

5. Sample Example: Blink an LED

Now, it's time to do our first Arduino project. In this example, we are going to make your Arduino board blink an LED.

Required Parts

- Arduino Uno Board R3
- Breadboard – half size
- Jumper WiresUSB Cable
- LED (5mm)
- 220 Ohm Resistor

Connect The Parts

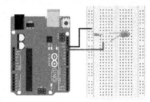

You can build your Arduino circuit by looking at the breadboard image above or by using the written description below. In the written description, we will use a letter/number combo that refers to the location of the component. If we mention H19 for example, that refers to column H, row 19 on the breadboard.

Step 1 – Insert black jumper wire into the GND (Ground) pin on the Arduino and then in the GND rail of the breadboard row 15.

Step 2 – Insert red jumper wire into pin 13 on the Arduino and then the other end into F7 on the breadboard.

Step 3 – Place the LONG leg of the LED into H7.

Step 4 – Place the SHORT leg of the LED into H4.

Step 5 – Bend both legs of a 220 Ohm resistor and place one leg in the GND rail around row 4 and other leg in I4.

Step 6 – Connect the Arduino Uno to your computer via USB cable.

6. Upload The Blink Sketch
Now it's time to upload the sketch (program) to the Arduino and tell it what to do. In the IDE, there are built-in example sketches that you can use which make it easy for beginners.

Arduino is case sensitive.
To open the blink sketch, you will need to go to File > Examples > Basics > Blink

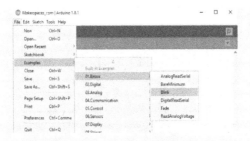

Now you should have a fully coded blink sketch that looks like the image below.

Next, you need to click on the verify button (check mark) that's located in the top left of the IDE box. This will compile the sketch and look for errors.

Once it says "Done Compiling" you are ready to upload it. Click the upload button (forward arrow) to send the program to the Arduino board.

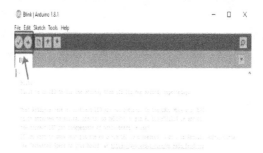

The built-in LEDs on the Arduino board will flash rapidly for a few seconds and then the program will execute. If everything went correctly, the LED on the breadboard should turn on for a second and then off for a second and continue in a loop.

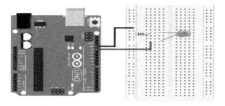

You have just completed your first Arduino project.

Change The Code
Before we go to the next project, lets change some of the code in the "Blink" sketch to make it do something different. Playing around with the sketch will help you start to learn how the code controls the board.

```
// the setup function runs once when you press reset or power the board
void setup() {
  // initialize digital pin LED_BUILTIN as an output.
  pinMode(LED_BUILTIN, OUTPUT);
}

// the loop function runs over and over again forever
void loop() {                          ← Changed to 200
  digitalWrite(LED_BUILTIN, HIGH);
  delay(200);
  digitalWrite(LED_BUILTIN, LOW);
  delay(200);
}                                      ← Changed to 200
```

Keep the Arduino board connected and change the delay portion of the code from (1000) to (200). Click the verify button on the top left of the IDE and then click upload. This should make the LED on the breadboard blink fast.

Chapter 7.
Implementing IoT Using RASPBERRY PI

The Raspberry Pi, unlike the Arduino, wasn't designed for physical comput-ing at all, but rather, for education. The vision of Eben Upton, trustee and cofounder of the Raspberry Pi Foundation, was to build a computer that was small and inexpensive and designed to be programmed and experimented with, like the ones he'd used as a child, rather than to passively consume games on. The Foundation gathered a group of teachers, programmers, and hardware experts to thrash out these ideas from 2006.

While working at Broadcom, Upton worked on the Broadcom BCM2835 system-on-chip, which featured an exceptionally powerful graphics process-ing unit (GPU), capable of high-definition video and fast graphics rendering. It also featured a low-power, cheap but serviceable 700 MHz ARM CPU, almost tacked on as an afterthought. Upton described the chip as "a GPU with ARM elements grafted on" (www.gamesindustry.biz/articles/digitalfoundry-inside-raspberry-pi).

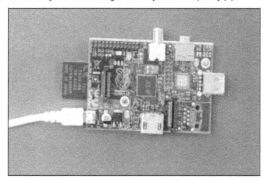

A Raspberry Pi Model B board. The micro USB connector only provides power to the board; the USB connectivity is provided by the USB host connectors (centre-bottom and centre-right).

The project has always taken some inspiration from a previous attempt to improve computer literacy in the UK: the "BBC Micro" built by Acorn in the early 1980s. This computer was invented precisely because the BBC producers tasked with creating TV programmes about programming realized that there wasn't a single cheap yet powerful computer platform that was suffi-ciently widespread in UK schools to make it a sensible topic for their show. The model names of the Raspberry Pi, "Model A" and "Model B", hark back to the different versions of the BBC Micro. Many of the other trustees of the Raspberry Pi Foundation, officially founded in 2009, cut their teeth on the BBC Micro. Among them was David Braben, who wrote the seminal game of space exploration, Elite, with its cutting-edge 3D wireframe graphics.

Due in large part to its charitable status, even as a small group, the Founda-tion has been able to deal with large suppliers and push down the costs of the components. The final boards ended up costing around £25 for the more powerful Model B (with built-in Ethernet connection). This is around the same price point as an Arduino, yet the boards are really of entirely different specifications.

So, the Raspberry Pi is effectively a computer that can run a real, modern operating system, communicate with a keyboard and mouse, talk to the Internet, and drive a TV/monitor with high-resolution graphics. The Arduino has a fraction of the raw processing power, memory, and storage required for it to run a modern OS. Importantly, the Pi Model B has built-in Ethernet (as does the Arduino Ethernet, although not the Due) and can also use cheap and convenient USB WiFi dongles, rather than having to use an extension "shield".

Note that although the specifications of the Pi are in general more capable than even the top-of-the-range Arduino Due, we can't judge them as "better" without considering what the devices are for! To see where the Raspberry Pi fits into the Internet of Things ecosystem, we need to look at the process of interacting with it and getting it to do useful physical computing work as an Internet-connected "Thing", just as we did with the Arduino! We look at this next.

However, it is worth mentioning that a whole host of devices is available in the same target market as the Raspberry Pi: the Chumby Hacker Board, the BeagleBoard, and others, which are significantly more expensive. Yes, they may have slightly better specifications, but for the price difference, there may seem to be very few reasons to consider them above the Raspberry Pi. Even so, a project might be swayed by existing hardware, better tool support for a specific chipset, or ease-of-use considerations. In an upcoming section, we look at one such board, the BeagleBone, with regards to these issues.

CASES AND EXTENSION BOARDS

Still, due to the relative excitement in the mainstream UK media, as well as the usual hacker and maker echo chambers, the Raspberry Pi has had some real focus. Several ecosystems have built up around the device. Because the Pi can be useful as a general-purpose computer or media centre without requiring constant prototyping with electronic components, one of the first demands enthusiasts have had was for convenient and attractive cases for it. Many makers blogged about their own attempts and have contributed designs to Thingiverse, Instructables, and others. There have also been several commercial projects. The Foundation has deliberately not authorised an "official" one, to encourage as vibrant an ecosystem as possible, although staffers have blogged about an early, well-designed case created by Paul Beech, the designer of the Raspberry Pi logo (http://shop.pimoroni.com/products/pibow).

Beyond these largely aesthetic projects, extension boards and other accesso-ries are already available for the Raspberry Pi. Obviously, in the early days of the Pi's existence post launch, there are fewer of these than for the Arduino; however, many interesting kits are in development, such as the Gertboard (www.raspberrypi.org/archives/tag/gertboard), designed for conveniently playing with the GPIO pins.

Whereas with the Arduino it often feels as though everything has been done already, in the early days of the Raspberry Pi, the situation is more encourag-ing. A lot of people are doing interesting things with their Pis, but as the platform is so much more high level and capable, the attention may be spread more thinly—from designing cases to porting operating systems to working on media centre plug-ins. Physical computing is just *one* of the aspects that attention may be paid to.

DEVELOPING ON THE RASPBERRY PI

Whereas the Arduino's limitations are in some ways its greatest feature, the number of variables on the Raspberry Pi are much greater, and there is much more of an emphasis on being able to do things in alternative ways. How-ever, "best practices" are certainly developing. Following are some sugges-tions at time of writing. (It's worth checking on the Raspberry Pi websites, IRC channels, and so on, later to see how they will have evolved.)

If you want to seriously explore the Raspberry Pi, you would be well advised to pick up a copy of the Raspberry Pi User Guide, *by Eben Upton and Gareth Halfacree (Wiley, 2012).*

Operating System

Although many operating systems can run on the Pi, we recommend using a popular Linux distribution, such as

Raspbian: Released by the Raspbian Pi Foundation, Raspbian is a distro based on Debian. This is the default "official" distribution and is certainly a good choice for general work with a Pi.

Occidentalis: This is Adafruit's customized Raspbian. Unlike Raspbian, the distribution assumes that you will use it "headless"—not connected to keyboard and monitor—so you can connect to it remotely by default. (Raspbian requires a brief configuration stage first.)

For Internet of Things work, we recommend something such as the Adafruit distro. You're most probably not going to be running the device with a keyboard and display, so you can avoid the inconvenience of sourcing and setting those up in the first place. The main tweaks that interest us are that

The sshd (SSH protocol daemon) is enabled by default, so you can connect to the console remotely.

The device registers itself using zero-configuration networking (zero-conf) with the name raspberrypi.local, so you don't need to know or guess which IP address it picks up from the network in order to make a connection.

When we looked at the Arduino, we saw that perhaps the greatest win was the simplicity of the development environment. In the best case, you simply downloaded the IDE and plugged the device into the computer's USB. (Of course, this elides the odd problem with USB drivers and Internet connec-tion when you are doing Internet of Things work.) With the Raspberry Pi, however, you've already had to make decisions about the distro and down-load it. Now that distro needs to be unpacked on the SD card, which you purchase separately. You should note that some SD cards don't work well with the Pi; apparently, "Class 10" cards work best. The class of the SD card isn't always clear from the packaging, but it is visible on the SD card with the number inside a larger circular "C".

At this point, the Pi may boot up, if you have enough power to it from the USB. Many laptop USB ports aren't powerful enough; so, although the "On" light displays, the device fails to boot. If you're in doubt, a powered USB hub seems to be the best bet.

An Electric Imp (left), next to a micro SD card (centre), and an SD card (right).

After you boot up the Pi, you can communicate with it just as you'd commu-nicate with any computer—that is, either with the keyboard and monitor that you've attached, or with the Adafruit distro, via ssh as mentioned previously. The following command, from a Linux or Mac command line, lets you log in to the Pi just as you would log in to a remote server:

$ ssh root@raspberrypi.local

From Windows, you can use an SSH client such as PuTTY (www.chiark. greenend.org.uk/~sgtatham/putty/). After you connect to the device, you can develop a software application for it as easily as you can for any Linux computer. How easy that turns out to be depends largely on how comfortable you are developing for Linux.

Programming Language

One choice to be made is which programming language and environment you want to use. Here, again, there is some guidance from the Foundation, which suggests Python as a good language for educational programming (and indeed the name "Pi" comes initially from Python).

Let's look at the "Hello World" of physical computing, the ubiquitous "blinking lights" example:

```
import RPi.GPIO as GPIO from time import sleep
GPIO.setmode(GPIO.BOAR  numbering    scheme
D) # set the                to be the
                     same
#                   as   on the board
GPIO.setup(8,       set   GPIO pin 8 to output
GPIO.OUT)  #        the   mode

led = False
PIO.output(8, led)  # initiate the LED to off
while 1: GPIO.output(8, led)
led = not led # toggle the LED status on/off for the next     # iteration
sleep(10)      #     sleep for     one second
```

As you can see, this example looks similar to the C++ code on an Arduino. The only real differences are the details of the modularization: the GPIO code and even the sleep() function have to be specified. However, when you go beyond this level of complexity, using a more expressive "high-level" language like Python will almost certainly make the following tasks easier:

Handling strings of character data
Completely avoiding having to handle memory management (and bugs related to it)
Making calls to Internet services and parsing the data received Connecting to databases and more complex processing

Abstracting common patterns or complex behaviours
Also, being able to take advantage of readily available libraries on PyPi (https://pypi.python.org/pypi) may well allow simple reuse of code that other people have written, used, and thoroughly tested.

So, what's the catch? As always, you have to be aware of a few trade-offs, related either to the Linux platform itself or to the use of a high-level programming language. Later, where we mention "Python", the same considerations apply to most higher-level languages, from Python's contem-poraries Perl and Ruby, to the compiled VM languages such as Java and C#. We specifically contrast Python with C++, as the low-level language used for Arduino programming.

Python, as with most high-level languages, compiles to relatively large (in terms of memory usage) and slow code, compared to C++.

The former is unlikely to be an issue; the Pi has more than enough memory. The speed of execution may or may not be a problem: Python is likely to be "fast enough" for most tasks, and certainly for anything that involves talking to the Internet, the time taken to communicate over the network is the major slowdown. However, if the electronics of the sensors and actuators you are working with require split-second timing, Python might be too slow. This is by no means certain; if Bubblino starts blowing bubbles a millisecond later, or the DoorBot unlocks the office a millisecond after you scan your RFID card to authenticate, this delay may be acceptable and not even noticeable.

Python handles memory management automatically. Because handling the precise details of memory allocation is notoriously fiddly, automatic memory management generally results in fewer bugs and performs adequately. However, this automatic work has to be scheduled in and takes some time to complete. Depending on the strategy for garbage collection, this may result in pauses in operation which might affect timing of subsequent events.

Also, because the programmer isn't exposed to the gory details, there may well be cases in which Python quite reasonably holds onto more memory than you might have preferred had you been managing it by hand. In worse cases, the memory may never be released until the process terminates: this is a so-called memory leak. Because an Internet of Things device generally runs unattended for long periods of time, these leaks may build up and eventually end up with the device running out of memory and crashing. (In reality, it's more likely that such memory leaks happen as a result of programming error in manual memory management.)

Linux itself arguably has some issues for "real-time" use. Due to its being a relatively large operating system, with many processes that may run simultaneously, precise timings may vary due to how much CPU priority is given to the Python runtime at any given moment. This hasn't stopped many embedded programmers from moving to Linux, but it may be a consideration for your case.

An Arduino runs only the one set of instructions, in a tight loop, until it is turned off or crashes. The Pi constantly runs a number of processes. If one of these processes misbehaves, or two of them clash over resources (memory, CPU, access to a file or to a network port), they may cause problems that are entirely unrelated to your code. This is unlikely (many well-run Linux computers run without maintenance for years and run businesses as well as large parts of the Internet) but may result in occasional, possibly intermittent, issues which are hard to identify and debug.

We certainly don't want to put undue stress on the preceding issues! They are simply trade-offs that may or may not be important to you, or rather more or less important than the features of the Pi and the access to a high-level programming language.

The most important issue, again, is probably the ease of use of the environ-ment. If you're comfortable with Linux, developing for a Pi is relatively simple. But it doesn't approach the simplicity of the Arduino IDE. For example, the Arduino starts your code the moment you switch it on. To get the same behaviour under Linux, you could use a number of mechanisms, such as an initialization script in /etc/init.d.

First, you would create a wrapper script—for example, /etc/init.d/ StartMyPythonCode. This script would start your code if it's called with a start argument, and stop it if called with stop. Then, you need to use the chmod command to mark the script as something the system can run: chmod +x /etc/init.d/StartMyPythonCode. Finally, you register it to run when the machine is turned on by calling sudo update-rc.d StartMyPythonCode defaults.

If you are familiar with Linux, you may be familiar with this mechanism for automatically starting services (or indeed have a preferred alternative). If not, you can find tutorials by Googling for "Raspberry Pi start program on boot" or similar. Either way, although setting it up isn't hard per se, it's much more involved than the Arduino way, if you aren't already working in the IT field.

Debugging
While Python's compiler also catches a number of syntax errors and attempts to use undeclared variables, it is also a relatively permissive language (compared to C++) which performs a greater number of calculations at runtime. This means that additional classes of programming errors won't cause failure at compilation but will crash the program when it's running, perhaps days or months later.

Whereas the Arduino had fairly limited debugging capabilities, mostly involving outputting data via the serial port or using side effects like blinking lights, Python code on Linux gives you the advantages of both the language and the OS. You could step through the code using Python's integrated debugger, attach to the process using the Linux strace command, view logs, see how much memory is being used, and so on. As long as the device itself hasn't crashed, you may be able to ssh into the Raspberry Pi and do some of this debugging while your program has failed (or is running but doing the wrong thing).

Because the Pi is a general-purpose computer, without the strict memory limitations of the Arduino, you can simply use try... catch... logic so that you can trap errors in your Python code and determine what to do with them. For example, you would typically take the opportunity to log details of the error (to help the debugging process) and see if the unexpected problem can be dealt with so that you can continue running the code. In the worst case, you might simply stop the script running and have it restart again afresh!

Python and other high-level languages also have mature testing tools which allow you to assert expected behaviours of your routines and test that they perform correctly. This kind of automated testing is useful when you're working out whether you've finished writing correct code, and also can be rerun after making other changes, to make sure that a fix in one part of the code hasn't caused a problem in another part that was working before.

SOME NOTES ON THE HARDWARE

The Raspberry Pi has 8 GPIO pins, which are exposed along with power and other interfaces in a 2-by-13 block of male header pins. Unlike those in the Arduino, the pins in the Raspberry Pi aren't individually labelled. This makes sense due to the greater number of components on the Pi and also because the expectation is that fewer people will use the GPIO pins and you are discouraged from soldering directly onto the board. The intention is rather that you will plug a cable (IDC or similar) onto the whole block, which leads to a "breakout board" where you do actual work with the GPIO.

Alternatively, you can connect individual pins using a female jumper lead onto a breadboard. The pins are documented on the schematics. A female-to-male would be easiest to connect from the "male" pin to the "female" breadboard. If you can find only female-to-female jumpers, you can simply place a header pin on the breadboard or make your own female-to-male jumper by connecting a male-to-male with a female-to-male! These jumpers are available from hobbyist suppliers such as Adafruit, Sparkfun, and Oomlout, as well as the larger component vendors such as Farnell.

The block of pins provides both 5V and 3.3V outputs. However, the GPIO pins themselves are only 3.3V tolerant. The Pi doesn't have any over-voltage protection, so you are at risk of breaking the board if you supply a 5V input! The alternatives are to either proceed with caution or to use an external breakout board that has this kind of protection. At the time of writing, we can't recommend any specific such board, although the Gertboard, which is mentioned on the official site, looks promising.
Note that the Raspberry Pi doesn't have any analogue inputs (ADC), which means that options to connect it to electronic sensors are limited, out of the box, to digital inputs (that is, on/off inputs such as buttons). To get readings from light-sensitive photocells, temperature sensors, potentiometers, and so on, you need to connect it to an external ADC via the SPI bus. You can find instructions on how to do this at, for example, http://learn.adafruit.
com/reading-a-analog-in-and-controlling-audio-volume-with-the-raspberry-pi/overview.
We mentioned some frustrations with powering the Pi earlier: although it is powered by a standard USB cable, the voltage transmitted over USB from a laptop computer, a powered USB hub, or a USB charger varies greatly. If you're not able to power or to boot your Pi, check the power requirements and try another power source.

OPENNESS

Because one of the goals of the Raspberry Pi is to create something "hack-able", it is no surprise that many of the components are indeed highly open: the customized Linux distributions such as "Raspbian" (based on Debian), the ARM VideoCore drivers, and so on. The core Broadcom chip itself is a proprietary piece of hardware, and they have released only a partial data-sheet for the BCM2835 chipset. However, many of the Raspberry Pi core team are Broadcom employees and have been active in creating drivers and the like for it, which are themselves open source.
These team members have been able to publish certain materials, such as PDFs of the Raspberry Pi board schematics, and so on. However, the answer to the question "Is it open hardware?" is currently "Not yet" (www.raspberrypi.
org/archives/1090#comment-20585).

The Raspberry Pi is a pocket-friendly and pocket-sized version of a Central Processing Unit, complete with a processor, memory and RAM among other components. Originally developed in the UK, the rpi was intended to act as a means to provide processing power to those individuals for whom the traditional computers were way too costly or just out of reach. It, thus, opened up a new gateway of possibilities to the common user, thereby creating a revolution of its own in the field of technology.

Implementation of IoT using Raspberry Pi

The Raspberry Pi is a pocket-friendly and pocket-sized version of a Central Processing Unit, complete with a processor, memory and RAM among other components. Originally developed in the UK, the rpi was intended to act as a means to provide processing power to those individuals for whom the traditional computers were way too costly or just out of reach. It, thus, opened up a new gateway of possibilities to the common user, thereby creating a revolution of its own in the field of technology.

Recent innovations of various RPi models have led to a promising start of an affordable yet powerful, automated system that can be applied in multiple domains. Showing some serious potential for smart-systems, the RPi may hold the key to creating efficient, autonomous computing sub-systems.

The capabilities of this wonderful device, however, are not restricted to automation only. The GPIO (General Purpose Input/output) in particular, is a very crucial part of the RPi. It allows the attaining of useful information through a logical data-flow mechanism and processes it to decide the RPi's response. It consists of various pins that provide a means to connect the necessary hardware with the RPi. This paper presents a basic application of RPi in the field of home automation and Internet of Things, in which the control signal of the respective GPIO pin of the Raspberry Pi is controlled by the status of the appliance stored in a MySQLite Database table as binary values which is read by the Python script that is run on the RPi continuously as soon as it boots. The interfaces used to change the status of the appliance in the database are a custom-made Android App or a web-page.

This status value is stored in the database as 0 or 1.Depending on this value, the appliance is either turned ON or OFF. The purpose of the python script, here, is to manipulate the signal via GPIO and set it as either high or low based on user-action through the Android App or Web-browser. A multimeter is used to effectively check the actual status (ON/OFF) of the GPIO pins in the RPi and thus, confirm that the device is working successfully.

Getting started with the Windows 10 IoT Core on Raspberry Pi

The Raspberry Pi is a small computer that can do lots of things. We can plug it into a monitor and attach a keyboard and mouse.

March 14 is known as Pi Day because the date represents the first three numbers in the mathematical constant π (3.14). We're celebrating with our coverage of everything Raspberry Pi related. If you've never even thought of what HTML means, you can still create amazing gadgets using Raspberry Pi and a bit of imagination.

Step 1: Get the Board and Tools Ready
The things required are-

1. A PC running Windows 10

2. Raspberry Pi Model A/B/B+

3. Raspberry Pi 5v Micro USB power supply with at least 1.0A current. If you plan on using several power-hungry USB peripherals, use a higPher current power supply instead (>2.0A).

4. 8GB Micro SD card – class 10 or better.

5. HDMI cable and monitorEthernet

6. CableMicroSD card reader – due to an issue with most internal micro SD card readers,

we suggest an external USB micro SD card reader.

Step 2: Install the Windows 10 IoT Core Tools

1. Download a Windows 10 IoT Core image from this Download page. Save the ISO to a local folder on your desktop/laptop.

2. Double click on the ISO (Iot Core RPi.iso). It will automatically mount itself as a virtual drive so you can access the contents.

3. Install Windows_10_IoT_Core_RPi2.msi. When installation is complete, flash.ffu will be located at C:\Program Files (x86)\Microsoft IoT\FFU\RaspberryPi2.

4. Eject the Virtual CD when installation is complete – this can be done by navigating to the top folder of File Explorer, right clicking on the virtual drive, and selecting "Eject".

Step 3: Put the Windows 10 IoT Core Image on Your SD Card
1. Insert a Micro SD Card into your SD card reader.

2. Use IoTCoreImageHelper.exe to flash the SD card. Search for "Windows IoT" from

start menu and select the shortcut "WindowsIoTImageHelper".

3. The tool will enumerate devices as shown. Select the SD card you want to flash, and then provide the location of the ffu to flash the image.

NOTE: IoTCoreImageHelper.exe is the recommended tool to flash the SD card.

4. Safely remove your USB SD card reader by clicking on "Safely Remove Hardware" in your task tray, or by finding the USB device in File Explorer, right clicking, and choosing "Eject". Failing to do this can cause corruption of the image.

Step 4: Plug in Board

1. Insert the micro SD card you prepared into your Raspberry Pi 2 (the slot is indicated by arrow #1 in the image below).

2. Connect a network cable from your local network to the Ethernet port on the board.

3. Make sure your development PC is on the same network.

4. Connect an HDMI monitor to the HDMI port on the board.

5. Connect the power supply to the micro USB port on the board.

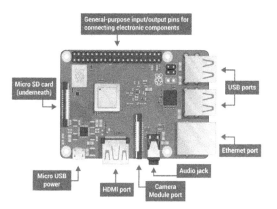

USB ports – these are used to connect a mouse and keyboard. You can also connect other components, such as a USB drive.

SD card slot – you can slot the SD card in here. This is where the operating system software and your files are stored.

Ethernet port – this is used to connect the Raspberry Pi to a network with a cable. The Raspberry Pi can also connect to a network via wireless LAN.

Audio jack – you can connect headphones or speakers here.

HDMI port – this is where you connect the monitor (or projector) that you are using to display the output from the Raspberry Pi. If your monitor has speakers, you can also use them to hear sound.

Micro USB power connector – this is where you connect a power supply. You should always do this last, after you have connected all your other components.

GPIO ports – these allow you to connect electronic components such as LEDs and buttons to the Raspberry Pi.

Step 5: Boot Windows 10 IoT Core

1. Windows 10 IoT Core will boot automatically after connecting the power supply. This process will take a few minutes. After seeing the Windows logo, your screen may go black for about a minute – don't worry, this is normal for boot up. You may also see a screen prompting you to choose a language for your Windows 10 IoT Core device – either connect a mouse and choose your option, or wait about a 1-2 minutes for the screen to disappear.

2. Once the device has booted, the DefaultApp will launch and display the IP address of your RPi2.

Step 6: Connecting to Your Device

1.You can use Windows Device Portal to connect to your device through your favorite web browser. The device portal provides configuration and device management capabilities, in addition to advanced diagnostic tools to help you troubleshoot and view the real time performance of your Windows IoT Device.

NOTE: It is highly recommended that you update the default password for the Administrator account.

Step 7: Finish Off

Now you should be ready with a windows 10 raspberry pi.

Browsing the web

You might want to connect your Raspberry Pi to the internet. If you didn't plug in an ethernet cable or connect to a WiFi network during the setup, then you can connect now.

Click the icon with red crosses in the top right-hand corner of the screen, and select your network from the drop-down menu. You may need to ask an adult which network you should choose.

- Type in the password for your wireless network, or ask an adult to type it for you, then click **OK**.

- When your Pi is connected to the internet, you will see a wireless LAN symbol instead of the red crosses.

- Click the web browser icon and search for `raspberry pi`.

When your Pi is connected to the internet, you will see a wireless LAN symbol instead of the red crosses.

Click the web browser icon and search for raspberry pi.

Creating a Raspberry PI app with Visual Studio on Windows 10 IoT Core

This article demonstrates how to build and debug a simple Raspberry PI application using Visual Studio. Earlier we have seen the seen and install Windows 10 IoT Core on Raspberry pi 3.

1. Download (http://gnutoolchains.com/raspberry) Windows toolchain for Raspberry PI and install it by running the installer on your desktop (Windows 10).

2. If you have not prepared the SD card yet, download and unpack (http://downloads.raspberrypi.org/raspbian_latest) the SD card image.

3. Go to the directory where you have installed the toolchain and run **tools\WinFLASHTool.exe**

4. Specify the path to the SD card image you have downloaded and unpacked.

5. Insert your SD card into the card reader and select it in the list:

6. Press the Write button. Double-check the information in the confirmation dialog to avoid confusing the SD card with another storage device and rewriting it by mistake:

7. Wait until WinFLASHTool finishes writing the image to your SD card. Writing the SD card typically takes several minutes depending on the card speed:

8. Insert the SD card into the slot on the Raspberry PI board. Connect the network cable to connect it with desktop. Optionally connect the keyboard and the HDMI cable. Finally connect the power cable and let the board start:

9. Use the

keyboard/screen (ifconfig command) or the DHCP status viewer of your router to find out the IP address of the Raspberry PI board. In this tutorial it is **192.168.0.114**

10. Please download (https://visualgdb.com/download)and install the latest VisualGDB on your desktop which is compatible with **Visual Studio 2008-19.**

11. On your Windows machine start Visual Studio, select "File->New project". Then select "VisualGDB->Linux Project Wizard". Specify project location and press "OK".

12. The VisualGDB Linux Project Wizard will start. As we are making a simple "Hello, World" application, keep "Create a new project" selected and press "Next".

13. If you have not created any Raspberry PI projects before, select "Create a new SSH connection" on the next page.

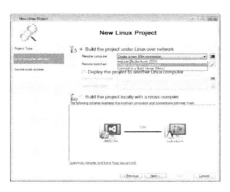

14. Provide the IP address of your Raspberry PI box, the user name ("pi" by default) and password ("raspberry" by default). It is recommended to check the "setup public key" checkbox, so that VisualGDB will automatically generate an public/private keypair, store it in your Windows account's key container and setup the Raspberry PI box to use it.

If you don't enable public key authentication, VisualGDB will remember your password for this connection. The stored passwords are encrypted using a key stored in your Windows account. Thus, the password will only be available once you login using your Windows account.

15. You could use 2 options to build your first Raspberry PI app: build it on Windows with a cross-compiler or build it on the Raspberry PI itself. The first option is faster, while the second is easier to setup. In this tutorial we will use the second option:

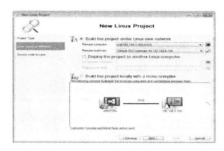

Use the diagram at the bottom of the page to check the correctness of your setup:
a. The hammer icon corresponds to the machine
where the compiler is run.
b. The "play" icon corresponds to the machine where the debugged program is launched.

16. When you press "Next", VisualGDB will test your toolchain by trying to compile and run a trivial program. If any errors are detected at this stage, you will see a detailed error log with further troubleshooting information.

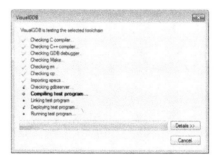

17. As the same source code will be edited under Windows and then compiled under Linux, VisualGDB will need to keep the sources synchronized. The easiest way is to use

automatic file uploading via SSH.

18. Press Finish to complete the wizard. If this is your first project for Raspberry PI, VisualGDB will cache the include directories to make them available through IntelliSense.

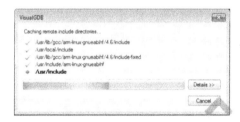

19. Replace the contents of the main source file with the following:

```
1  #include <stdio.h>
2  #include <unistd.h>
3
4  int main(int argc, char *ar
5  {
6      char szHost[128];
7      gethostname(szHost, si
8      printf("The host name
9      return 0;
10 }
```

20. Build the solution. You will see how the source files are transferred to Raspberry PI and compiled there:

21. Set a breakpoint on the printf() line and press F5 to start debugging. The breakpoint will trigger:

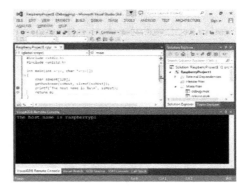

22. VisualGDB provides an advanced Clang-based IntelliSense engine that is fully compatible with GNU language extensions and provides advanced features like refactoring, Code Map and auto completion in the Watch windows:

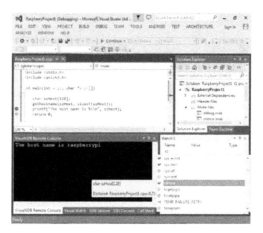

23. You can customize various project settings by right-clicking on the project in Solution Explorer and selecting VisualGDB Project Properties:

You can now use all normal Visual Studio techniques to debug your app.

SMART PREMISES

Internet of Things

The Internet of Things (IoT) , in its most basic form, can be described as a system comprised of various "things" that are interconnected to each other for the sole purpose of creating, sending, manipulating and processing data.

A thing, in this definition, could be any device, machine, object, or an organism capable of doing one or all of the aforementioned tasks. Although it was perceived as an idea quite a long time ago, the IoT did not officially come into the picture of technological advancements until the 90's which was also around the same time that there was a major boom in the devices using Internet and the web itself.

With the popularity of the Internet and the public welcoming various new horizons of the modern world into their daily life, it became possible for both commercial and non-commercial developers and innovators to create devices and systems that were previously not explored, either due to being unpopular or having limited functionality. But now, every device that was on the Internet was in one way or another, part of an IoT system without even realizing it. The model of the World Wide Web was actually synonymous with a spider's web and it could be said that each device that was connected, was passing information on the web that could be used by another device on the web to perform certain tasks. But, this group of connected devices would need to be logical, in order to work as an efficient system.

For example, integrating the temperature sensor in your room to your AC system would be a nice touch of automation. But, trying to integrate the garage door system with your bathtub would make no sense at all. The key here is trying to understand, which of the systems or sub-systems would benefit through integration and which ones are better left alone. Once we are able to identify this, we regulate the data flow from one-device to another and hence, create a chain of linked devices, that can not only function as individual entities, but also work as a module of a group to generate new data and perform operations based on input from other similar devices. In essence, we create an IoT system that can work autonomously or have some extent of control by waiting for user-action to do something.

Premise Automation

The concept of a fully automated, smart premise is one of the most popular technologies out there in the world which has been praised by both the Common User and Tech Gurus alike. The sudden increase in the development and innovation of such systems/sub-systems, of course, is due to the extent of control and ease we have gained from the Internet.

With the Internet growing into an ever expanding Universe of more and more people joining it per second, we have also started using the Internet for more than just a Google search or posting our favorite moments for others to see. The true potential of the Internet lies in the amount of data that it can generate and support in terms of the processing power and storage facilities among others. Connecting and controlling multiple devices by adding them to a common interface that flows through all of them seamlessly, is pretty much the definition of the IoT and when combined with multiple platforms like Web and Android, we can further stretch the limits of what such a system can achieve through a simple User-Action. This connection and control is not confined to a few devices, however. With the right kind of tools, we can grow this feature by moving into premise automation.

An automated/smart premise (like a Smart Home or Smart Hotel) is pretty much a physical area consisting of multiple electronic-devices that we use in our daily lives. No matter what the size or purpose of the device is, if it is on the grid and connected to its peers, you can control it remotely with a few simple actions ranging from a simple hand gesture to a complete biometric authentication.

The most uncomplicated example of this, though, is the one described below, where a User can control multiple devices using one touch or click.

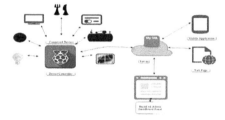

Software Implementation

The RPi runs on Raspbian O.S. which is based on the Debian Wheezly Linux O.S. and uses a Python script to operate the appliances connected to it. The user has the following two interface options to send device data to the database in real-time which is read by the Python script continuously on the RPi :

Web Page

For development of the web-page implemented on the user-end, HTML5 & JavaScript were used. On the server-end we have PHP to read static data containing information about the GPIO ports that are in use and the devices connected to each room in JSON format. The web-page offers control of remote devices via three main interfaces which are as follows :

Login Form : The login form is a simple PHP script that interacts with a MySQLite database. On successful login, the user can see a screen that lets him/her select a room.

Screen For Selecting A Room : On this screen, the user selects a room of their choice from the entire premise layout available. As soon as the user does this, he/she will get a pop-up to enter credentials provided to them at the time of registration (like hotel check-ins etc). The following information is stored about the rooms in JSON format:
   Room Name/Room No
   Description
   Type
Each room is represented by a JSON object containing the above mentioned data for each room.

Devices : This screen shows the information about the room selected in the previous screen and all the connected devices in the room. Each individual device is represented by an icon that displays the type, name, description and status of that device. Other than these, there will be two separate operational buttons attached to each device. These two buttons will be labeled ON and OFF and used to remotely turn a particular device ON or OFF.

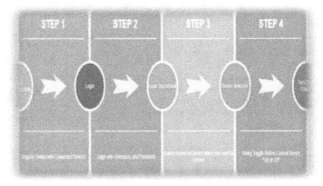

Android Application

The working of the Android Application is similar in function to the web-page to some extent. Initially, the user has to login to the app using a login screen. After the successful login of user, he/she will be asked for an extra credential provided at the time of registration. After this authentication, the user will be able to see the selected room of their choice. The room will further contain icons/images representing various devices that are interconnected to each other inside the room. The device that is selected by user will display certain information like type, name, description and status of the device. The device status can be manipulated by using one of the two toggle buttons labeled ON and OFF respectively for each individual device. The user will then toggle one of the two buttons to send status value for that device to the MySQLite database via the PHP script.The data gathered from the User action through any of the two interfaces (Web , or Android) will ultimately be passed on to the MySQLite database and later read by the Python script running continuously on the RPi to actually switch ON or OFF the device.

Hardware Implementation

The integration of electronic components into the Raspberry-pi we have used are: Raspberry Pi 3 Model B, power supply module for Raspberry Pi, 830 Tie Points MB102 Breadboard, Bulb, 8 Channel DC 5V Relay Module for RPi, Smartphone, a internet connection for both Smartphone and Raspberry Pi.

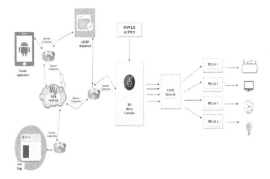

OTHER APPLICATIONS

There some more really interesting areas where the RPi can be implemented. Following is a list of such possible applications of RPi :

2. Remote Camera: When connected to a camera, the RPi has the ability to transmit images to end-user remotely by responding to an event or command initiated by the user.

3. Chat Bot: The ability of the RPi to accept and respond to content from the end user makes it an ideal candidate for its implementation as a bot. To make things further interesting, you can also create another bot instead of an actual user sending data to the RPi.

4. Digital Advertisement Screen: The RPi can also be used to display digitally created advertisements like video/animation etc by simply connecting it to a display device or a projector. Any change in display screen we can edit or operate remotely by owner/user from anywhere, anytime using internet.

5. Android TV: Another interesting application of the RPi is that you can turn your regular TV into an Android TV by simply integrating it with an RPi having an Android TV operating system.

6. Automated Printer Machine: One of the most innovative ideas is to create a smart photo-copy/printing machine that accepts all parameters like number of pages, print format etc from the user, along with a payment for the photo-copy/print and automatically prints the required number of pages for the customer. It would even display messages like out of ink/paper etc. Also we can add credentials (like Barcode Reader, RFID card) to the machine for authenticating a free user or employee in the system.

7. Customizable Device: The RPi can be customized to create multi-purpose systems like a visual device such as a Tablet and personalized audio-video systems that include a combination of various display screens and audio-cards. Also, the RPi can be tweaked to create a streaming device for your network requirements with a highly -configurable design.

Physical Computing Device: The RPi can serve the purpose of a physical computing device that interacts with the outside world using many digital/virtual projects like home media centers, arcade gaming centers or custom-made servers

Chapter 8.
Introduction - Edge Computing

Concept

Historically, network architectures and computing models have oscillated between the use of shared and central resources, and exclusive and local compute power. As of today, available massive distributed deployments of sensors and intelligent devices known as the internet of things (IoT) are confronted with the currently dominating cloud computing model emphasizing centralized shared resources. This model challenges the increasing use of mobile applications and use cases utilizing local resources and information gained from them.

Edge computing is a distributed open platform at the network edge, close to the things or data sources, integrating the capabilities of networks, storage, and applications. By delivering edge intelligence services, edge computing meets the key requirements of industry digitalization for agile connectivity, real-time services, data optimization, application intelligence, security and privacy protection.

Serving as a bridge between the physical and digital worlds, edge computing enables smart assets, smart gateways, smart systems, and smart services.

Edge intelligence is born

The concept of edge intelligence (EI) introduces a paradigm shift with regard to acquiring, storing, and processing data: the data processing is placed at the edge between the data source (e.g. a sensor) and the IoT core and storage services located in the cloud. As such, the literal definition of edge and intelligence specified in Figure 1-1 is adopted: the ability to acquire and apply knowledge and skills is shifted towards the outside of an area, here, the core communication network or the cloud.

EI allows bringing data (pre-)processing and decision-making closer to the data source, which reduces delays in communication. In addition, such (pre-)processing makes it possible to accumulate and condense data before forwarding it to IoT core services in the cloud or storing it, which perfectly matches the capacities offered by the upcoming fifth generation wireless technology (5G) networks providing localized throughput and delay enhancements.

Basic Characteristics and Attributes

• Connectivity
Connectivity is the basis of edge computing. The diversity of connected physical objects and application scenarios requires that edge computing provide abundant connection functions such as various network interfaces, protocols, topologies, network

deployment and configuration, and network management and maintenance. Connectivity needs to fully draw on the advanced research achievements in the network field, such as TSN, SDN, NFV, NaaS, WLAN, NB-IoT, and 5G. Additionally, connectivity needs to consider interoperability with a variety of existing industrial buses.

• First Entry of Data
As a bridge between the physical and digital worlds, edge computing is the first entry of data. With mass, real-time, and complete data, edge computing implements data management and creates values based on the data E2E lifecycle, supporting innovative applications such as predictive maintenance, asset efficiency and management. In addition, as the first entry of data, edge computing also faces the challenges caused by real-time, determinacy, and diversity.

• Constraint
Edge computing products need to adapt to harsh working conditions and operating environments at industrial sites, such as anti-electromagnetic interference, anti-dust, anti-explosion, anti-vibration, and anti-current/voltage fluctuations. Moreover, in industrial interconnection scenarios, high requirements are imposed on the power consumption, cost, and space of edge computing devices.

Edge computing products need to be integrated and optimized through hardware and software to adapt to various conditions and constraints and support diverse scenarios of industry digitalization.

• Distribution
In actual deployment, edge computing needs to support distributed computing and storage, achieve dynamic scheduling and unified management of distributed resources, support distributed intelligence, and deliver distributed security capabilities.

• Convergence
Convergence of the Operational Technology (OT) and Information and Communications Technology (ICT) is an important foundation for the digital transformation of industries. As the key carrier of "OICT" convergence and collaboration, edge computing must support collaboration in connection, data, management, control, application, and security.

"CROSS" Value of Edge Computing

• Mass and Heterogeneous Connection
Networks are the cornerstone of system interconnection and data aggregation transmission. With the surge in the number of connected devices, networks face enormous challenges in terms of Operations and Maintenance (O&M), management, flexible expansion, and reliability. In addition, a large number of heterogeneous bus connections have long existed at industrial sites, and multi-standard industrial Ethernet coexists. It is a tough issue that must be solved to achieve compatibility among multiple connections and ensure real-time reliability of connections.

- Real-Time Services
Industrial system testing, control, and implementation have high real-time requirements, even within 10 milliseconds in some scenarios. If data analysis and control logic is are implemented only on the cloud, it is difficult to meet the real-time requirements of services.

- Data Optimization
Today, industrial sites contain a large amount of heterogeneous data. Data optimization must be implemented for data aggregation and unified presentation and openness, so that the data can serve intelligent edge applications in a flexible and efficient manner.

- Smart Applications
Business process optimization, O&M automation, and service innovation drive applications to be smart. Edge intelligence delivers significant efficiency and cost advantages. Intelligent applications represented by predictive maintenance are driving industries to transition to new service models and business models.

- Security and Privacy Protection
Security is critical to cloud and edge computing, requiring end-to-end protection. The network edge is close to Internet of Things (IoT) devices, making access control and threat protection difficult. Edge security includes device security, network security, data security, and application security. The integrity and confidentiality of key data, as well as protection of mass production or personal data are also key areas of focus for security.

Collaboration of Edge Computing and Cloud Computing

Figure 8.1: Edge & Cloudlets

Cloud computing is suitable for non-real-time, long-period data and business decision-making scenarios, while edge computing plays an irreplaceable role in scenarios such as real-time, short-period data and local decision-making.

Edge and cloud computing are two important foundations for the digital transformation of industries. The collaboration between them in respect of network, service, application, and intelligence will help support more scenarios and unleash greater value in industry digitalization.

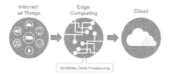

Figure 8.2: 1 Points of collaboration between edge computing and cloud computing

Point of Collaboration	Edge Computing	Cloud Computing
Network	Data aggregation (TSN + OPCUA)	Data analysis
Service	Agent	Service orchestration
Application	Micro applications	Lifecycle management of applications
Intelligence	Distributed reasoning	Centralized training

Edge Computing Scenario

Volume versus available bandwidth

Devices and sensors can produce more data than is economically feasible to transmit to the cloud. To address this problem, analytical algorithms can be applied at the edge to process the incoming sensor data and only send higher level events to the core.

For example, tens or hundreds of cameras produce video streams at 60 frames per second. Even with compression, the transmission of video streams can be very costly. A video analysis service could be deployed at the edge that identifies people, objects (e.g. vehicles), and their properties (e.g. license plates and x,y coordinates). Only this higher level information would then be sent to the core.

The video content would be stored locally at the edge for a certain duration and could be accessed by a human operator for further analysis as needed.

IoT solutions are often cost sensitive, and communication costs specifically represent a significant portion of ongoing expenses. Low bandwidth wide area protocol solutions, such as LoRA, Sigfox and others, can reduce the communication cost. But these solutions come with the unwanted consequences associated with low bandwidth, such as reduced performance.

Thus, communication costs can be addressed more effectively by using analytical algorithms to process the incoming sensor data and only send alerts (another form of higher level events) to the core. This also enables confidential or privacy related data to be kept near the data source so that the disclosure of data can be limited.

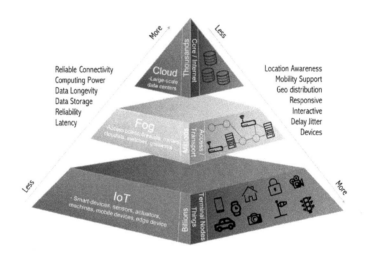

Figure 8.3: Edge Scenario

Comparing Fog Computing with Edge Computing

With the proliferation of mobile and connected devices, massive volume velocity of data is being generated with high velocity. According to Gartner, *there will be more than 20.4 billion connected devices all over the world by 2020.*
As the data explodes, cloud wouldn"t be enough to handle the flood of information, devices, and interactions. Cloud computing allows easier access to compute, for storage and connectivity. However, it works as a centralized resource which can result in delays to act on data.

When an internet of things (IoT) device generates data, it is sent back for processing to a centralized cloud or data centrer source. But by the time this data is processed, the chance to act on it might no longer exist.

For example, if the temperature of a chemical tank is about to cross its acceptable limit, the action will need to be taken within seconds. A connected device will send the data to the cloud for analysis, and by the time everything gets done, there will be no opportunity to prevent a spoiled batch.

Edge computing and fog computing are the technologies that can address this problem. These technologies push capabilities of processing and intelligence at the source of data generation , rather than sending it to the cloud or data centre. The main difference between edge computing and fog computing is exactly where the processing power and intelligence are pushed.

Edge computing

Computing which happens close to the or near to source of data generation, rather than depending on a centralized cloud for data processing, is called edge computing.

Also known as edge, the eEdge computing (also known as edge) eliminates the time and distance required to send data to the cloud. It doesn''t mean that there is no need for cloud. It means that the cloud comes to the device. This enhances speed and performance for transporting the data, along with devices and applications on the edge.

Edge computing has the potential to enable dynamic communication among several things. Imagine a driverless car sending data for processing to the cloud, which may take a long time to analyzse data. This may result in accidents. Edge computing seeks to accommodate that. It will process data in real-time at the car itself.

The global edge computing market will reach $3.24 billion by 2025, according to a recent report by Million Insights.

Fog computing

Fog computing involves bringing intelligence to local area network architecture and processing the data in a fog node.
Concept of fog computing was given by Cisco in 2014. According to Cisco, *fog computing is a standard that defines the way edge computing should work, and it enables the operation of compute, storage and networking services between end devices and cloud computing data centeres.*
What this means is that it works as a layer to define the location of data generation and the location of that data to be stored, like cloud or customer''s data centrer.

Edge computing vs fog computing

Data generated from IoT devices can be processed at three locations: cloud, network, or device itself. As mentioned above, if data is processed in the cloud, it will take a lot of time to get analyszed. So, it is better to process it either on the network or in the device.

Both the technologies bring intelligence and data to analytics platforms located close to the source of data generation, like speakers, motors, screens, sensors, etc. The aim of these technologies is to reduce latency issues, while depending on the cloud to analyzse data and make quicker data-driven decisions.

So, what is the difference between edge computing and fog computing?

The key difference between fog computing and edge computing is associated with the location where the data is processed.

In edge computing, the data is processed right on the devices, or gateway devices closest to the sensors. So, the compute and storage systems are located at the edge, close to device, application, or component producing the data.

Whereas, in fog computing, the edge computing happenings processing isare moved to processors linked to a local area network or into the hardware of LAN. Therefore, the data in fog computing is processed within an IoT gateway or fog node in LAN.

Long story short: eEdge computing places the intelligence in the connected devices themselves, whereas, fog computing puts it in the local area network.

<u>Advantages of edge computing and fog computing</u>
    Real-time data analysis: Since, the data is processed at the source of data generation, it can be analyzsed in real-time or near real-time.
    Reduced costs: These technologies lower the costs as companies need less data bandwidth management solutions for local devices, as compared to the cloud or data centrer.
    Lower bandwidth consumption: Companies wouldn"t need high bandwidth to handle data, because processing will happen at the edge itself.
    Lower latency levels: This is the main benefit of edge computing and fog computing. They lower the latency compared to a faraway cloud or data centrer by eliminating the time involved in sending data back and forth.

<u>Applications of edge computing</u>
Oil and gas industry
Edge computing holds a key role in the oil and gas industry. Several IoT devices are deployed to monitor temperature, humidity, pressure, moisture and many other factors. The data generated from these devices provides insights about the health of the systems.

Analyszing and processing the data in real-time helps the industry to prevent several incidents.

Intelligent transportation and traffic management
IoT technology is being used to effectively manage traffic and transportation. Since, the traffic data is gathered using sensors and cameras, it needs to be acted upon in real-time, otherwise it will be of no use. Edge computing processes massive amounts of

data on the traffic hardware itself, while reducing operational and storage costs.

Self-driving vehicles
Although, the self-driving vehicles have not become the norm, but edge computing is a necessary technology for them. It will be impossible for such vehicles to work, without analyszing data in real-time.

Driverless vehicles host artificial intelligence and IoT applications at the edge, so that latency levels between data generated and used to run vehicles is extremely low.

Applications of fog computing
Smart cities
There are a lot of challenges for large cities, like public safety, traffic congestion, high energy usage, municipal services, etc. Fog computing can help in addressing these challenges by deploying a network of fog nodes, forming a single IoT network.

Many cities are failing to transform into smart ones, because of broadband bandwidth and connectivity issues. Deployment of fog nodes can optimize the bandwidth, while providing local storage and processing.

Smart buildings
To make large buildings smarter, thousands of sensors will be needed for measuring several parameters like keycard readers, temperature, occupancy of parking space, etc. Fog computing can be implemented in such buildings for autonomous operations.

The smart buildings will have fog nodes on each floor to monitor the functions, control lights and other electric appliances, etc. It will also provide compute and storage infrastructure to complement capabilities of mobile devices.

For example, a sensor will generate data when it senses smoke, and then process it to fog nodes in real-time for further actions.

Visual security
For security purposes, cameras are installed everywhere in public places like parking lots, shopping malls, restaurants, etc. The data from these cameras require high storage and bandwidth to carry it to the cloud. Also, it can"t be analyszed in real-time.

By implementing a fog computing architecture, the video processing for sensitive surveillance systems can be divided between fog nodes. This can enable real-time tracking and detection of anomalies or any other such activities.

Companies working on fog computing development
The leading companies from the cloud industry who had a collective vision that fog computing can transform IoT and other digital concepts, founded a joint ecosystem for it. Called OpenFog Consortium, the ecosystem was founded in 2015 by Arm Holdings, Cisco, Dell, Intel, Microsoft, and Princeton University.

Since then, many large organizations, startups, research institutions and universities have joined the OpenFog Consortium. The contributing members of the OpenFog include Foxconn, Hitachi, Sakura Internet, and Shanghai Tech University, etc-etc.

COMPATABILITY OF CLOUD, FOG AND EDGE COMPUTING

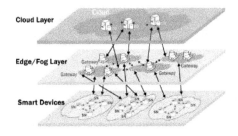

Figure 8.4: Compatibility of Cloud, Fog and Edge

Organizations that rely heavily on data are increasingly likely to use cloud, fog, and edge computing infrastructures. These architectures allow organizations to take advantage of a variety of computing and data storage resources, including the Industrial Internet of Things (IIoT). Cloud, fog and edge computing may appear similar, but they are different layers of the IIoT. Edge computing for the IIoT allows processing to be performed locally at multiple decision points for the purpose of reducing network traffic. Industrial embedded computer systems can leverage the power of the IIoT to enable the successful design of high-performing industrial applications.

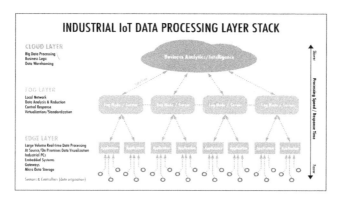

Figure 8.5: Layer Stack

Cloud Computing

Most enterprises areu familiar with cloud computing since it's now a de facto standard in many industries. Fog and edge computing are both extensions of cloud networks, which are a collection of servers comprising a distributed network. Such a network can allow an organization to greatly exceed the resources that would otherwise be available to it, freeing organizations from the requirement to keep infrastructure on site. The primary advantage of cloud-based systems is they allow data to be collected from multiple sites and devices, which is accessible anywhere in the world.

Embedded hardware obtains data from on-site IIoT devices and passes it to the fog layer. Pertinent data is then passed to the cloud layer, which is typically in a different geographical location. The cloud layer is thus able to benefit from IIoT devices by receiving their data through the other layers. Organizations often achieve superior results by integrating a cloud platform with on-site fog networks or edge devices. Most enterprises are now migrating towards a fog or edge infrastructure to increase the utilization of their end-user and IIoT devices.

The use of embedded systems and other specialized devices allows these organizations to better leverage the processing capability available to them, resulting in improved network performance. The increased distribution of data processing and storage made possible by these systems reduces network traffic, thus improving operational efficiency. The cloud also performs high-order computations such as predictive analysis and business control, which involves the processing of large amounts of data from multiple sources. These computations are then passed back down the computation stack so that it can be used by human operators and to facilitate machine-to-machine (M2M) communications and machine learning.

Fog Computing

Fog computing and edge computing appear similar since they both involve bringing intelligence and processing closer to the creation of data. However, the key difference between the two lies in where the location of intelligence and compute power is placed. A fog environment places intelligence at the local area network (LAN). This architecture transmits data from endpoints to a gateway, where it is then transmitted to sources for processing and return transmission. Edge computing places intelligence and processing power in devices such as embedded automation controllers.

For example, a jet engine test produces a large amount of data about the engine's performance and condition very quickly. Industrial gateways are often used in this application to collect data from edge devices, which is then sent to the LAN for processing.

Fog computing uses edge devices and gateways with the LAN providing processing capability. These devices need to be efficient, meaning they require little power and produce little heat. Single-board computers (SBCs) can be used in a fog environment to receive real-time data such as response time (latency), security and data volume, which can be distributed across multiple nodes in a network.

Edge Computing

The IoT has introduced a virtually infinite number of endpoints to commercial networks. This trend has made it more challenging to consolidate data and processing in a single data center, giving rise to the use of "edge computing." This architecture performs computations near the edge of the network, which is closer to the data source.

Edge computing is an extension of older technologies such as peer-to-peer networking, distributed data, self-healing network technology and remote cloud services. It's powered by small form factor hardware with flash-storage arrays that provide highly optimized performance. The processors used in edge computing devices offer improved hardware security with a low power requirement. Industrial embedded SBCs and data acquisition modules provide gateways for the data flow to and from an organization's computing environments.

The IIoT is composed of edge, fog and cloud architectural layers, such that the edge and fog layers complement each other. Fog computing uses a centralized system that interacts with industrial gateways and embedded computer systems on a local area network, whereas edge computing performs much of the processing on embedded computing platforms directly interfacing to sensors and controllers. However, this distinction isn't always clear, since organizations can be highly variable in their approach to data processing.

Edge computing offers many advantages over traditional architectures such as optimizing resource usage in a cloud-computing system. Performing computations at the edge of the network reduces network traffic, which reduces the risk of a data bottleneck. Edge computing also improves security by encrypting data closer to the network core, while optimizing data that's further from the core for performance. Control is very important for edge computing in industrial environments because it requires a bidirectional process for handling data. Embedded systems can collect data at a network's edge in real time and process that data before handing it off to the higher -level computing environments.

Conclusion

The growth of the IIoT has increased the need for edge, fog, and cloud platforms. Embedded systems that can be utilized in industrial environments to enable solutions for edge computing requirements and gateways within the fog platforms. Embedded systems thus allow us to leverage our particular IIoT hardware and network infrastructure.

Chapter 9.
The evolution of computing models towards edge computing

Shared and central resources versus exclusive and local computation

The computing models of the last seven decades are now oscillating between the use of shared and central resources or exclusive and local compute power. Key factors in deciding the direction of the curve are advances in computing and communication. Cheap and powerful compute power pushes towards the use of local resources. Cheap and fast communication technologies enable the use of shared, central resources.

Models which relied heavily on shared resources included mainframes operated in batch mode or which were controlled by text-only terminals. At the opposite end of the spectrum, the standalone personal computers (PCs) of the 1980s were powered by affordable compute power.

Networked PCs and client-server models created a more balanced computing model between the two extremes enabled by high-speed local area networks.

The pendulum swung back towards central resources with the early web model enabled by cheap and fast wide area networking, compared to the level of data being transferred.

Today"s dominating cloud computing model still emphasizes centralized shared resources, but mobile apps and JavaScript-heavy web applications often make good use of local resources.

Shared and centralized resources are highly efficient, as they maximize the utilization of compute resources and provide elasticity. Given their central location, typically in data centres, they can be more easily secured, and their lifecycle management is less complex than in distributed systems. However, they need highly available communication channels of sufficient bandwidth and speed to reach end users, which may incur significant cost.

Exclusive and local resources can work in isolation, but the compute power, memory and storage are limited and may be insufficient for certain tasks.

As such devices are often under end user control, securing and managing them, as well as the lifecycle of their applications, becomes more complex.

The cloud computing model seems to have found a happy compromise in the distributed computing spectrum, balancing the pros and cons between exclusive/local versus shared/central, but this solution will not last.

IoT disrupts the cloud

The IoT disrupts the cloud compute model by introducing new usage scenarios resulting in the following key requirements:

- Real-time: oOften, decisions need to be made within tens of milliseconds. Today"s communication infrastructure and the laws of physics require local decision-making, as a roundtrip to the cloud would take an excessive amount of time.

- Connectivity: tToday's mobile networks are often spotty and cannot guarantee connectivity to the cloud. Hence, decision-making must occur locally.

- Data volume: tThe amount of data generated by sensors can be huge;, for example, hundreds of high-resolution cameras creating video streams at 30 frames per second, which could clog wide-area communication channels.

- Context: tThe business context needed for interpreting IoT data for decision-making is typically held in centralized enterprise systems.

The disruption of the cloud model is not the displacement of the cloud but rather its extension to the edge.

Characteristics of the new computing model

The cloud will continue to exist. For example, certain functions are best performed in the cloud, such as the training of predictive analytics algorithms, as typically only the cloud holds the necessary data in its entirety.

Devices will have compute and storage capabilities;, for instance, high-end security cameras can store and analyzse videos on the device.

Edge computing will provide compute power and storage in the space between the device and the cloud. Edge compute devices include IoT gateways, routers, and micro data centres in mobile network base stations, on the shop floor and in vehicles, among other places.

The new model will be a fully distributed computing model. It will support a wide range of interaction and communication paradigms, including the following:

- Autonomous, local decision-making based on incoming IoT data and cached enterprise information

- Peer-to-peer networking, for example, security cameras communicating amongst themselves about an object within their scope

- Edge networking, for example, platoon driving, i.e. vehicles self-organizing into groups which travel together, orchestrated and controlled by a micro data centre in the base station of a mobile network

- Distributed queries across data that is stored in devices, in the cloud and anywhere in between

• Distributed data management, for example, data aging: which data to store, where and for how long

• Self-learning algorithms that learn and execute on the edge, or learn in the cloud and execute on the edge, or learn and execute in the cloud

• Isolation, involving devices which are disconnected for a long time, operating on minimal energy consumption to maximize lifespan

Through the introduction of intelligence at the edge nodes, systems can:

• take decisions more quickly and efficiently, as the roundtrip delay in contacting the cloud is removed;

• reach decisions according to local identity management and access control policies, securing the data close to its source;

• reduce communication costs by limiting communication over public wide area networks.

The opportunities come from technology evolutions in manufactured devices and 5G networks, along with concepts, algorithms and Standards in software-defined networking, mobile edge computing, analytics and device and data ownership.

Blueprint of edge computing intelligence

Definition and high level architecture

This defines EI as the infrastructure nodes that span from devices, corporate networks and public or dedicated networks up to the cloud deployments of the service.
This means that several IT and OT technologies can be placed so close to the edge of the network that aspects such as real-time networks, security capabilities to ensure cybersecurity, self-learning solutions and personalized/customized connectivity can be addressed. This radical transformation from the cloud to the edge will support trillions of sensors and billions of systems and will treat data in motion differently from data at rest.

Application areas

IoT
From a network architecture perspective, the core of such an IoT solution is typically a central IT system, bearing the name of IoT core server, in charge of storing, processing and analyszing IoT data (, see Figure 2-2). Much of this IoT data often can be located in the cloud, away from the core.

IoT endpoints (i.e. devices with sensors and/ or actuators) frequently do not have the communication capabilities to transmit all their sensor data in a secure, reliable and cost-efficient manner to the core. The most common obstacles to such transmission include the following:

- Sensors may only support low energy ⬚protocols to conserve battery power.

- Mobile devices leveraging cellular⬚ communication lack coverage in certain locations.

- Mobile communication links are often ⬚bandwidth-constrained or expensive.

- Wide area connections can introduce too⬚ much latency for real-time decision-making.

Furthermore, certain local systems, for example, self-driving vehicles, must autonomously make decisions in real-time and cannot wait for instructions sent from the cloud.

EI can address these challenges. An IoT gateway is an example of an ECN. It connects to devices that are located away from the core (often referred to as 'devices "at the edge'") via communication protocols such as low-energy Bluetooth or ZigBee. At the same time, it also connects to the core directly using high-speed internet. Additionally, gateways provide security and lifecycle management at the edge, such that the edge is a sustainable and manageable compute unit. The hardware used for such gateways ranges from high-powered, rack-mounted servers to smaller devices with embedded processors, and anything in between.

IoT edge computing refers to the capability of processing, storing, and analyzsing sensor data as well as performing decision-making at ECNs.

The role of the ECN is:

1. To retrieve or pull IoT data from endpoints and content of a varied nature (e.g. media, enterprise bound, maps) from the IoT core servers, in order to be able to undertake data and networking analytics, take decisions on current information and self-adapt the local knowledge;
2. Based on the decision taken, to trigger an action towards the endpoints (e.g. actuate or change the threshold) or even send notifications towards the IoT core servers, e.g. request resources in terms of core computing, networking quality of service or dispatch of rescue forces, in case of fire or other dangerous situations.

Analysts, for example, the International Data Corporation (IDC), indicate that 40% of IoT-created data will be subject to IoT edge computing, and that this ratio of edge-to-core data and processing is growing annually [3].

Content delivery networks

A content delivery network (CDN) is a distributed network of servers bringing content to end users. The goal of a CDN is to optimize content delivery with high availability and performance, while minimizing required bandwidth in the backbone and saving transportation costs. Instead of using a centralized server at a single location, content is delivered from servers situated near to the endpoints. With CDNs, the traditional client-server model is split into two communication flows: one between end user and proxy media server and the other from the media server to the central server.

The advantages of CDNs include reduction of latency, limiting the impact of server and network failures and minimizing wide area transportation costs. A CDN also strengthens security. By being highly distributed, it can absorb the effects of less-sophisticated malicious attacks. The deployment of a CDN plays an essential role in the business strategy of content providers, leading to an improvement in the quality of experience of the customers. Enhancing user satisfaction represents a key factor for high conversion rates in online business, i.e. the number of website visitors actually performing desired actions such as purchase, subscription or ad-clicks.

CDN technology especially supports the delivery of large media files and streaming content, but other sites with heavy traffic that serve a large widely geographically distributed user community, e.g. social media or e-commerce in general, also benefit from CDNs.

Today CDNs serve a large fraction of the internet content. Such content may consist of web objects (text, graphics and scripts), downloadable objects (media files, software, documents), applications (e-commerce, portals), traffic from social networks and especially on-demand streaming media and live streaming media. A number of major companies specialize in the provisioning of CDN services, but support of CDN has also become part of the portfolio of global cloud services providers, internet service providers (ISPs) and network operators.

CDNs are derived from technologies for website acceleration, including server farms and intelligent caching. The CDN market started to develop in the late 1990s triggered by higher demand for audio and video streaming and growing volumes of content. With the further development of the technologies, additional factors such as cloud computing, energy awareness and user demand for more interactivity came into focus. Flash crowd phenomena observed in the context of events such as the 9/11 terrorist attacks created awareness concerning the importance of CDN solutions. The need for CDN services generated initiatives aimed at developing Standards for delivering broadband content and streaming rich media content (video, audio and associated data) over the internet.
The recent evolution of CDNs has been strongly driven by the continuing trend toward mobile end devices combined with a user expectation of receiving performance at least equal to conventional fixed or stationary devices. For creating a personalized interactive user experience, dynamic content generation needs to be supported with individually created suggestions and offers, without compromising download times and page rendering. As CDNs become increasingly sophisticated, the integration of multiple CDNs from different providers is often required.

CDNs form a major use case for increased EI. Media content is becoming even more localized, real-time and bandwidth-intensive. Hence, more intelligence at the edge is needed to address these challenges.

Tactile internet

The capability to transmit touch in perceived real-time, which is enabled by suitable robotics and haptics equipment at the edges together with an unprecedented communications network, is often referred to as the "tactile internet" [4]. Thus, tactile internet stands for near real-time human-machine interaction, including cases in which the human is mobile. The use cases and opportunities enabled by the tactile internet are numerous and the performance requirements of networks are highly demanding.

The latency requirements for the tactile internet are very challenging, with a round trip delay of 1 ms or less typically required. 4G mobile networks can offer about a 25 ms latency under ideal conditions, which is way off the 1 ms mark required. 5G promises to deliver ultra-low latency for a number of critical use cases, including industry automation, robotics, remote surgery, etc. Such latency can only be achieved by deploying new hardware in the air interface as well as through deployment of edge clouds. Furthermore, such latency requirements dictate the maximum distance from the sensor to the mobile edge cloud, restricted by the speed of light.

The use of edge clouds is necessary to fulfil the latency requirements of the tactile internet. However, edge clouds are also required in order to provide storage and computation for tactile internet services. Scalability, security and reliability are highlighted as critical characteristics of such edge computing in order to serve use cases such as remote surgery and industry automation, which are described below. The deployment options of edge real-time feedback is imperative to ensure clouds which determine a number of factors, including that a process or endpoint is operating scalability and latency by correctly deploying small cloudlets. Currently such systems are hard or very close to radio base stations which can be wired, for example, industrial Ethernet.

Chapter 10.
Mobile-Edge Computing

Mobile cloud computing

In recent years, we are witnessing significant demand for from users for to have different types of cloud services on their mobile devices;. Ffor instance, services in entertainment, social networking, business, news, games or health and well being. However, this demand results infaces mobile devices facing with issues like low energy, poor resources and low connectivity. To address this, the term Mobile Cloud Computing (MCC) came to light and researchers try to define the boundaries and give proper definitions.

There are several existing definitions for Mobile Cloud Computing. In general, it is a running service on a resource rich cloud server which is used by a thin mobile client. It can also be referred when mobile nodes play the role ofas a resource provider role in a peer-to-peer network. We can take the need for adaptability, scalability, availability and self-awareness in cloud computing concept and expand it to mobile cloud computing.

Mobile cloud computing inat its simplest form, refers to an infrastructure where both the data storage and data processing happen outside of the mobile device. Mobile cloud applications move the computing power and data storage away from mobile phones and into the cloud, bringing applications and MCC to not just smartphone users but a much broader range of mobile subscribers".

MCC tackles certain challenges of mobile devices in a desirable manner. Energy efficiency is reached by several solutions like intelligent access to disk or screen. In addition, data storage capacity and processing power areis improved through storing and accessing big data on the cloud. Also, we can have more reliability by storing our data on the cloud on different cloud servers.

However, despite of all improvements by MCC, there are still issues to be addressed. Issues like low bandwidth, high latency, service availability, quality of service (QoS) and service cost. Bandwidth is limited in wireless networks compared to normal wired networks. Users need high availability despite mobile devices' lack of connectivity and they demand better QoS and lowerless service cost. Moreover, network latency is still a big burden in improving user experience by getting the way of cloud services. These matters are more tangible in applications that virtual reality services which demand low latency and high bandwidth.

Therefore, considering the previously discussed weaknesses, utilizing re-sources in user proximity and improving the locality of services seems to improve the availability, connectivity and network latency.

Cloudlets

As it is depicted in Figure 10.1, cloudlet is considered as the middle tier of a 3-tier hierarchy: mobile device, cloudlet and cloud. A cloudlet can also be viewed as a resource rich centrer at the proximity of users. Cloudlet is connected to a larger cloud server and its goal is bring the cloud services closer to the end-user.

In the cloudlet concept, mobile device offloads its workload to a resource-rich, local cloudlet. Cloudlets would be situated in common areas such as coffee shops, libraries or university halls, so that mobile devices can connect and function as a thin client to the cloudlet. A cloudlet could be any first hop element at the edge of network while it has four key attributes. It has only soft state, it should be resource rich and well-connected, with low end-to-end latency and also it follows a certain standard for offloading (e.g. Virtual machine migration). In other words, a cloudlet's failure is not critical;, it has strong internal connectivity and high bandwidth wireless LAN and it should be in logical and physical proximity of the user to reduce the network latency.

There are two main approaches to implement cloudlet infrastructure using Virtual Machine (VM) technology. In both of these architectures, it is important that cloudlet could go back to its beginning state after being used (e.g. by post-use clean up). A VM based approach is broadly used since it can cleanly encapsulate and separate the transient guest software environment from the cloudlet infrastructure's permanent host software and it's less brittle than other approaches like process migration or software virtualization.

Regarding implementation, it should be possible to transfer a VM state from the user's mobile application to cloudlet's infrastructure. The first approach is VM migration in which an already executing VM is suspended and its state of processor, disk and memory will be transferred to destination and execution will be resumed from exact state of suspension in the cloudlet host environment. The second approach is dynamic VM synthesis which mobile device delivers a small VM overlay - instead of the mentioned states in first approach - to cloudlet infrastructure that possesses the VM base. The overlay is calculated by mobile device based on the customized image encapsulating the requirements of the application. Then the overlay is executed in the exact state that it was suspended and the result will be returned by the cloudlet.

Cloudlets utilize rapidly deployed VMs which the client can customize freely upon their need to make the VM image or VM overlay which has the application and all necessary requirements to run properly. In both types

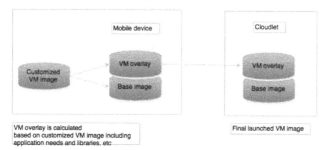

Figure 10.2: Cloudlet dynamic VM synthesis

of implementations, the VM image or overlay is created at runtime by the user which is quite exible for overloading the workload to the cloudlet. Nevertheless, despite this exibility, the procedure of creating an image or a VM overlay and also application status encapsulation could be quite time takingconsuming. At the end, it is totally dependeant on applicat135n design, needs and environment whether to choose using cloudlets as resource rich sources or not.

Mobile-Edge computing

Yet after all, it is notable that the business model of cloudlets isare not clear. In other words, who's going to play the role of network edge? Is it going to be only dedicated to private clouds which have the possibility of deploying cloudlets in their local network? Is there going to be any standards to increase the simplicity and also to encourage developers to create useful applications?

Realizing the advantages of bringing cloud services and resources closer, the cloudlet concept got the attention of Radio Access Network (RAN) operators, as it is a reasonably valid idea to use RAN base stations as the very first hop of network edge to serve mobile users. Hence, serious efforts have begun to make this idea practical for business environment. As an example, recently Nokia Networks introduced their new generation of intelligent base stations which are considered as edge computing platform enabled base stations (known as: **Nokia Radio Application Cloud Server (RACS)).**

Furthermore, ETSI (European Telecommunications Standards Institute) with cooperation of operators such as Huawei, IBM, Intel, Nokia Networks, NTT DOCOMO and Vodafone has formed an Industry Specification Group (ISG) to create a standardized and open environment platform for bringing cloud services closer to the end-users and to formulate a logical integration of mobile applications on such platform between vendors, service providers and third party developers. In other words, the objective is to create an initiative for Mobile-Edge Computing (MEC).

In ETSI's executive briefing, MEC is defined as follows:

"Mobile-edge Computing offers application developers and content providers cloud-computing capabilities and an IT service environment at the edge of the mobile network. This environment is characterized by ultra-low latency and high bandwidth as well as real-time access to radio network information that can be leveraged by applications."

MEC's goal is to transform base stations into high performance customiz-able intelligent service hubs on the edge of mobile networks while it generates revenue and unique value for operators from offering different value propositions to mobile users, such as proximity of resources, context and location awareness, agility and speed .

A MEC-enabled base-station provides developers with the ability of running an application on the network edge using a predefined standard platform. This platform might also offer some extra services such as cloud storage, caching, computing, etc to the application. Practically, this turns the base-station into a MEC server. A MEC server can be deployed at different types of LTE (Long-Term Evolution) base stations such as ENodeB or 3G RNC (Radio Network Controller). Figure 3.3 illustrates the general architecture of MEC.

To conclude, MEC is a new ecosystem which enables MNOs to provide authorized third - parties with a platform to access RAN edge and deploy unique applications based on MEC features. Finally, these advantages enhance quality of experience (QoE) for mobile subscribers and bring value for operators, letting them to play complementary and profitable roles within their respective business models.

Nokia Networks Solution to MEC

To keep pace with the trend of evolution in mobile base-stations, Nokia Networks recently announced their new generation of intelligent base-stations.

These base-stations are equipped with Nokia Networks Radio Applications

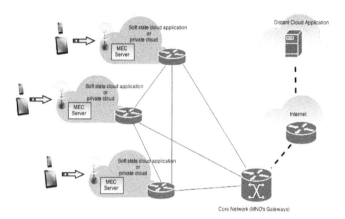

Figure 10.3: Architecture of Mobile-Edge Computing

Cloud Servers (RACS). RACS has both capabilities of a radio base-station and a MEC cloud server. Cloud applications can be developed on the RACS by third party developers and mobile users can get serviced by these applications while they are connected to one RACS.

On the RACS, applications are encapsulated and run in a virtual machine (VM) on the top of Nokia Networks application engine (, see fFigure 10.4). Each VM is customized according to the requirements of the application. When an application is deployed in Nokia Networks network, it means this customized VM is replicated on all the RACS. Each application with certain type of service is encapsulated in a different VM to keep applications from interfering with each other's services and also to make the run-time environment more secure. In Nokia Networks terminology, these applications are called Liquid Applications.

Regarding developers' point of view, Liquid Apps are distributed system applications and all the principles of distributed systems are valid in the environment. Particularly all the distributed system apps can be utilized and deployed on RACS. Nokia Networks has an application life cycle process for the third party developers. This process is called AppFactory. AppFactory consists of verification of the app idea, help and support in the development phase (e.g. test environment and simulation support), validation of developed app, publishing on the Nokia Networks RACS network and at the end,

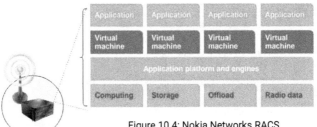

Figure 10.4: Nokia Networks RACS

maintenance. In other words, through the AppFactory process, developers can deploy their Liquid applications on RACS. After verification, development, test and validation phases, their app will be packaged into a customized VM and it will be deployed on all the RACS.

Chapter 11.
Edge Computing Reference Architecture

Model-Driven Reference Architecture

The reference architecture is designed based on Model-Driven Engineering (MDE) principles. The model used for the reference architecture enables knowledge in the physical and digital worlds to be modelled to achieve:

• Coordination Between the Physical and Digital Worlds

A real-time, systematic cognitive model of the physical world is established. The status of the physical world is predicted, and the running of the physical world emulated in the digital world. This approach simplifies reconstruction of the physical world and drives the physical world to optimize the operation of physical systems. Full lifecycle data of the physical world can coordinate with business process data to enable collaboration between business and production processes.

• Cross-Industry Collaboration

Based on the modelling approach, the Information and Communications Technology (ICT) industry and vertical industries can build and reuse knowledge modelling systems in their own realms. The ICT industry shields the complexity of ICT technologies using the horizontal edge computing model and reference architecture. Each vertical industry performs modelling encapsulation of the industry know-how, achieving effective collaboration between ICT vendors and vertical industries.

• Reduced System Heterogeneity and Simplified Cross-Platform Migration

Model-based interfaces between systems, subsystems, services, and new and legacy systems enable interaction, simplifying integration of these systems. Using the model, software interfaces can be decoupled from development languages, platforms, tools, and protocols, which reduces the complexity of cross-platform migration.

• Effective Support for System Lifecycle Activities

System lifecycle activities include full lifecycle activities of application development services, deployment and operation services, data processing services, and security services.

The ICT industry faces challenges such as the need to simplify architectures, establish service intelligence, and reduce Capital Expenditure (CAPEX) and Operating Expense (OPEX) in the areas of networking, computing, and storage. To address these challenges, the ICT industry is adopting technological innovations such as virtualization, Software-Defined Networking (SDN), model-driven Service Orchestrator (SO), and microservices. Edge computing is an Operation Technology (OT) and ICT convergence industry, and the edge computing reference architecture design needs to draw on the new technologies and concepts. In addition, edge computing and cloud computing coordinate with each other, yet differ in many ways. Therefore, edge computing faces unique challenges and requires unique and innovative technologies.

Based on the above concepts, the Edge Computing Consortium (ECC) proposes Edge Computing Reference Architecture 2.0.

From the horizontal perspective, the architecture has the following characteristics:

•	Smart services are based on the model-driven unified service framework. Intelligent coordination between service development and deployment is achieved through the development service framework and deployment & operation service framework. These frameworks enable consistent software development interfaces and automatic deployment and operations.

•	Smart service orchestration defines the E2E service flow through the service fabric (SF) to realize service agility.

•	Use of a Connectivity and Computing Fabric (CCF) enables a simplified architecture and simplifies the distributed edge intelligence architecture for services. The CCF also enables automatic and visualized deployment and operations of the OT & ICT (OICT) infrastructure, supporting coordination between edge computing resource services and service needs of industries.

•	Intelligent Edge Computing Nodes (ECNs) are compatible with a variety of heterogeneous connections, support real-time processing and response, and deliver integrated hardware and software security.

Edge Computing Reference Architecture 2.0 provides model-based open interfaces at each layer, enabling full-layer openness. Vertically, the architecture uses management services, lifecycle data services, and security services to deliver smart services in the entire service process and full lifecycle.

Multi-View Display
Guided by international standards defined by ISO/IEC/IEEE 42010:2011, the architecture systematically addresses the industry's concerns about edge computing and presents solutions and frameworks. Edge Computing Reference Architecture 2.0 is demonstrated using the following views:

• Concept View
Describes the domain models and key concepts of edge computing.

• Function View
Describes the functions and design concepts of the development service framework, deployment and operation framework SF, CCF, and ECN in the horizontal direction, as well as of cross-layer open services, management services, lifecycle data services, and security services in the vertical direction.

• Deployment View
Describes the system deployment process and typical deployment scenarios.

In addition, the architecture needs to meet typical cross-industry, non-functional requirements, including real-time performance, certainty, and reliability. To this end, related technical solution recommendations are provided in the function view and deployment view.

Concept View

Smart edge computing assets, systems, and gateways are digitalized, network-based, and intelligent. They provide ICT resources such as networks, computing, and storage, and can be logically abstracted as ECNs.

To suit the typical application scenarios of ECNs, the architecture defines four types of ECN development frameworks. Each framework includes an operating system, functional modules, and integrated development environment to meet the needs of various scenarios.

Typical functions of ECNs include:

- Bus protocol adaptation
- Real-time connection
- Streaming real-time data analysis
- Sequential data access
- Policy execution
- Device plug-and-play
- Resource management

Development frameworks of ECNs include:

• Real-Time Computing System
For digital physical assets; meets the needs of real-time applications.

• Lightweight Computing System
For sensing terminals with limited resources; meets the needs of low power consumption.

• Smart Gateway System
Supports multiple network interfaces, bus protocols, and network topologies; enables interconnection of local edge systems; delivers local computing and storage capabilities; and enables interworking with cloud systems.

• Smart Distributed System
Based on a distributed architecture, this framework flexibly expands network, computing, and storage capabilities at the network edge; supports service-oriented dynamic resource management and scheduling; and enables interworking with cloud systems.

Edge Computing Domain Models

Edge computing domain models are defined from the ICT perspective of edge computing.

ECN product implementation:	
Product	**Typical Scenario**
ICT-converged gateway	Connection of elevators, smart street lamp
Independent controller	Industrial Programmable Logic Controller (PLC)
Embedded controller	Virtual Programmable Logic Controller (vPLC), robot
Sensing terminal	Computer Numerical Control (CNC), instrument
Distributed service gateway	Smart power distribution
Edge cluster (edge cloud)	Digital workshop

Figure 11.1: Concept view: full lifecycle-oriented models

• Models in the Design Phase
Define the IDs, attributes, functions, performance, and derivation and inheritance relationships of ECNs, providing valuable information for the deployment and operation phases.

• Models in the Deployment Phase
Include service policy and physical topology models. The service policy model describes service rules and constraints using a service language rather than machine language, allowing services to drive the edge computing infrastructure. The service policy model is reusable and changeable, enabling service agility.

• Models in the Operation Phase
Include the connection computing fabric model and operation load model. Based on these models, the system operating status can be monitored and optimized, and the deployment of loads optimized on the distributed edge architecture.

Through the model-driven unified service framework, edge computing domain models and vertical industry models can be mapped to each other and centrally managed. In this way, vertical industry models such as OPC Unified Architecture (OPC UA) and its ecosystem can be reused, allowing for easy integration of the edge computing reference architecture with industry platforms and applications.

Function View

ECN

Edge virtualization function (EVF)

Virtualization		Virtualization layer	
Layer			
	Network	Computing	Storage
Basic	Software-defined		
resource	networking		Time series
layer	(SDN)	Heterogeneous	database
		computing (HC)	(TSDB)
	Time-sensitive		
	networking (TSN)		

1) Basic Resource Layer
This layer includes network, computing, and storage modules.

• Network
SDN architectures separate a network's control plane from the forwarding plane to make the network programmable. When SDN is applied to edge computing, the network can support access to millions of network devices as well as flexible expansion, enabling efficient and low-cost automatic O&M. Additionally, this approach helps achieve network and security policy association and integration.

Network connections need to accommodate requirements for transmission time certainty and data integrity. Time-Sensitive Networking (TSN) series standards define unified technical specifications for key services such as real-time priorities and clocks. TSN is the future development direction of industrial Ethernet connectivity.

• Computing
Heterogeneous Computing (HC) is a crucial aspect of the computing hardware architecture at the network edge. Even as Moore's Law continues to hold true for breakthroughs in chip technologies, the popularity of IoT applications has brought explosive growth in information volume, and the application of Artificial Intelligence (AI) has increased computing complexity. These developments place higher requirements on computing capabilities. The types of data to be processed are also becoming more diversified. As a result, edge devices need to process both structured and unstructured data. In addition, as ECNs contain more compute units and different types of compute units, costs become a concern.

Therefore, a new computing architecture is proposed that combines compute units that handle different types of instruction sets and have different architectures, that is, heterogeneous computing. Such an architecture gives full play to the advantages of various compute units, achieving a balance between performance, cost, power consumption, and portability.

Additionally, a new generation of AI technology, represented by deep learning, needs new technical optimizations at the network edge. Currently, the processing of a single picture at the inference stage often requires more than 1 billion computations, so standard deep learning algorithms are obviously not suitable for embedded computing environments at the network edge. Ongoing optimization for deep learning in the industry includes top-down optimization, which compresses learned deep-learning models to reduce computational load at the inference stage. Bottom-up optimization that redefines an algorithm architecture oriented for edge-side embedded system environment is also being attempted.

• Storage

The digital world needs to keep track of the dynamics of the physical world in real time and store complete historical data in chronological order. A new generation of Time Series Database (TSDB) offers efficient storage for time series data (including information such as timestamps of the data). TSDBs need to support basic functions of time series data, such as fast write, persistence, and multi-dimensional aggregated query. To ensure data accuracy and completeness, TSDBs need to continuously add new time series data instead of updating the original data. These requirements raise the following challenges:

•   The time series data write function must support writing tens or hundreds of millions of data points per second.

•   The time series data read function must support packet aggregation operations on hundreds of millions of data values within seconds.

•   The cost-sensitive nature of most scenarios means that the top priority of TSDBs is to reduce the cost of mass data storage.

2) Virtualization Layer

Virtualization technology reduces system development and deployment costs, and has been adopted into embedded system applications from server applications. Typical virtualization technologies include the bare metal architecture and host architecture. In the bare metal architecture, virtualization-layer functions such as the hypervisor run directly on the system hardware platform, and then operating system and virtualization functions run under the hypervisor. In the host architecture, virtualization-layer functions run under the host operating system. The bare metal architecture has better real-time performance and is generally used by smart assets and smart gateways.

3) EVF Layer

Edge Virtualization Functions (EVFs) are software-based and service-based functions that are decoupled from a proprietary hardware platform. Based on virtualization technology, the hardware, system, and specific EVFs can be vertically combined based on services on the same hardware platform. In this manner, multiple independent service zones can be virtualized and isolated from each other. ECN's EVF service scalability reduces CAPEX and extends a system's lifecycle.

EVFs can be flexibly combined and orchestrated, and migrated and expanded on different hardware platforms and devices, enabling dynamic resource scheduling and service agility.

The EVF layer delivers the following basic services that can be tailored:
- Distributed CCF service
- OPC UA service
- Streaming real-time data analysis service
- TSDB service
- Policy execution service
- Security service

Key ECN Technologies:

1) SDN

SDN uses a completely different control architecture from traditional networks. It separates the network control plane from the forwarding plane, replaces the original distributed control with centralized control, and implements "software-defined" through open, programmable interfaces. SDN, as a new technology, changes the way a network is built and operated: building networks from an application perspective and operating networks using Information Technology (IT).

The SDN architecture includes controllers, southbound/northbound interfaces, and various application-layer applications and infrastructure-layer Network Elements (NEs). The most important part of the architecture is the SDN controller. It implements configuration and management of forwarding policies at the infrastructure layer and supports forwarding control based on multiple flow tables.

SDN's unique benefits for edge computing include:

• Mass Connections

SDN supports access to millions of network devices and flexible expansion. SDN also integrates and adapts to the management of multi-vendor network devices.

• Model-Driven Policy Automation

SDN provides flexible network automation and management frameworks; enables service-based infrastructure and service delivery functions; and implements plug-and-play smart assets, gateways, and systems. These capabilities greatly reduce the technical requirements for network administrators.

• E2E Service Protection

SDN delivers E2E tunnel services, such as Generic Routing Encapsulation (GRE), Layer 2 Tunneling Protocol (L2TP), Internet Protocol Security (IPSec), and Virtual Extensible LAN (VXLAN). SDN also optimizes Quality of Service (QoS) scheduling, helps meet key requirements such as E2E bandwidth and delay specifications, and implements edge-to-cloud service coordination.

• Lifecycle Management of Applications

SDN supports lifecycle management tasks such as application deployment, loading, update, uninstallation, and deletion. SDN also supports multi-application resource scheduling and management, including priority enforcement, security, and QoS.

• Architecture Openness

SDN opens centralized network control and network status information to smart applications so that they can flexibly and quickly drive network resource scheduling.

Edge computing SDN technology has been successfully applied to smart buildings, smart elevators, and many other industry scenarios.

2) TSN

Standard Ethernet technologies have been widely implemented, with advantages such as high transmission speed, flexible topology, long transmission distance, and cost-effectiveness. Meanwhile, due to constraints from the traditional Quality of Service (QoS) mechanism and the Carrier Sense Multiple Access with Collision Detection (CSMA/CD) mechanism, Ethernet technologies cannot meet key industry requirements for timeliness and determinism. The industry optimizes standard Ethernet technologies and offers commercial implementations of multiple industrial real-time Ethernet technologies. Consequently, a variety of industrial real-time Ethernet networks coexist, creating obstacles and challenges for interoperation.

In recent years, IEEE802.1 defined the TSN technical standards, aiming to promote standardization and interoperability of real-time Ethernet networks, and ultimately merging Operational Technologies (OT) and ICT using 'one network.' This also brings the following advantages:

•   Ensures determinism with μs-level latency and jitter of less than 500 ns.

•   Meets large bandwidth requirements for scenarios such as industrial machine vision, with interface bandwidth of larger than 1 Gbit/s.

•   Achieves reliable data transmission through multiple paths or redundant paths.

•   Coordinates with SDN technologies to achieve unified scheduling management of TSN and non-TSN networks.

TSN is designed to provide a unified low-latency queue scheduling mechanism, resource reservation mechanism, clock synchronization mechanism, path control mechanism, and configuration management model at the Media Access Control (MAC) layer of Ethernet networks, to achieve interoperation between TSN networks and standard Ethernet networks.

Currently, a good industrial collaboration ecosystem for TSN has been established. For example, IEEE is responsible for standards establishment, Avnu Alliance is responsible for interoperability certification, and industrial organizations represented by the ECC and the Industrial Internet Consortium (IIC) are performing industry demonstrations and promotion through test beds and other activities.

3) HC

Heterogeneous computing architecture is designed to coordinate and bring into play unique advantages of various computing units: The Central Processing Unit (CPU) manages system control, task decomposition, and scheduling; the Graphics Processing Unit (GPU) has strong floating-point and vector computing capabilities, and performs well with parallel computing such as matrix computing and vector computing; the Field Programmable Gate Array (FPGA) unit provides advantages such as hardware programmability and low latency; the

Application-Specific Integrated Circuit (ASIC) unit offers advantages such as low power consumption, high performance, and cost-effectiveness.

The objective of heterogeneous computing is to integrate separate processing units of the same platform to collaboratively execute different types of computing loads. Moreover, heterogeneous computing achieves cross-platform deployment of software through open, unified programmable interfaces.

The heterogeneous computing architecture uses the following key technologies:

• Memory processing optimization
With a traditional architecture, data transfer between different computing units requires data replication, which not only occupies processor resources, but also occupies a large amount of system bus bandwidth. Heterogeneous computing enables uniform memory access of multiple computing units. Data of any processing unit can be easily accessed by other processing units, without the need of copying the data to each other's memory area, which greatly improves system performance.

• Task scheduling optimization
The relationship of various computing units changes from master-slave relationship to equal partnership. The most appropriate computing unit is dynamically determined to execute the workload based on tasks. Heterogeneous computing involves a series of optimizations, including those of scheduling algorithms, instruction sets, and compilers.

• Tool chain for development
The tool chain provides application programmers with hardware and software interfaces as well as a basic runtime environment; encapsulates and hides complicated bottom-layer details such as memory consistency and task scheduling management; supports optimization of architecture parameters and task scheduling; and minimizes the application porting workload. For Artificial Intelligence (AI) applications, this tool chain integrates multiple open AI training and reasoning platforms and is compatible with multi-vendor computing units.

Heterogeneous computing is currently used in both chip design and edge computing platform design. In terms of chips, heterogeneous computing integrates CPU and GPU resources to accelerate video encoding and decoding. In terms of computing platforms, heterogeneous computing uses CPU and FPGA (or GPU) resources to achieve implementation of AI functions in areas such as smart transportation and smart robots.

4) Time Series Database (TSDB)

Efficient writing, query, and distributed storage of large amounts of data are key challenges to TSDBs. TSDBs use the following key technologies:

• Distributed storage
The core for distributed storage is how to distribute data to multiple machines, that is, data fragmentation. Data fragmentation can be implemented based on timestamps, tags, and priorities. Data fragments that have the same tag (one or more identical fields), are generated within the same time range, and matching priority conditions are stored on the same machine. Data can be compressed before it is stored, which improves data writing efficiency and saves storage space.

• Priority-based storage
Using timestamps of time series data as the priority division basis is very efficient. Data that was processed recently is queried for more times and is considered hot data. Data that was processed a long time ago is queried less often and is considered cold data. In addition, factors such as storage costs are often considered in priority-based storage. Data with different priorities is stored on storage media with different costs (including memories, HDDs, and SSDs).

• Fragment-based query optimization
During data queries, all data segments are queried based on query conditions. All of the fragments are merged based upon the timestamp conditions to generate the original data results. If the query conditions include aggregation operations on data, these operations are performed based on the time sampling window for returning the results.

Besides commercial versions, the industry has a large number of open-source TSDBs, such as OpenTSDB, KairosDB, and InfluxDB. In addition to meeting performance challenges, TSDBs need to provide industry data modelling and visualization tools and to support rapid integration with industry application systems.

Service Fabric

A service fabric is a model-based workflow that digitally represents service requirements. It consists of multiple types of logically related functional services that collaborate with each other to implement specific service requirements.
The service model includes the following information:
•   Service name
•   Function to be executed or provided
•   Nesting, dependency, and inheritance relationships between services
•   Input and output of each service
•   Service constraints such as QoS, security, and reliability

The service types include universal services provided by edge computing and specific industry services defined by vertical industries.

A service fabric has the following features:
•   Focus on service processes and shield technical details, helping service departments, development departments, and deployment operation departments establish effective cooperation.
•   Decouple from the OICT infrastructure and hardware platform to implement cross-technology platforms and support service agility.
•   As a service description model, it can be inherited and reused to implement fast modelling.

A service fabric provides the following functions:

•   Workflow and workload definition
•   Visualized display
•   Semantic check and policy conflict detection
•   Version management of fabric and service models

CCF

The CCF is a virtualized connectivity and computing service layer. It has the following features:

- Shield the heterogeneity between ECNs.
- Reduce the complexity of the smart distributed architecture in terms of data consistency and error tolerance.
- Implement the discovery, unified management, and orchestration of resource services.
- Support the sharing of data and knowledge models between ECNs.
- Support dynamic scheduling and optimization of the service load.
- Support distributed decision-making and policy execution.

A CCF provides the following functions:

a. Resource awareness
The CCF can detect the ICT resource status (such as network connection quality and CPU usage), performance specifications (such as real-time performance), and physical information (such as location) of each ECN, providing key input for resource allocation and scheduling at the edge.

b. EVF awareness
The CCF can detect the EVFs provided by the system, ECNs where the EVFs are distributed, computing tasks that each EVF serves, and task execution status.

c. Workload scheduling
The CCF supports proactive task scheduling. It can automatically divide the workload into multiple subtasks based on resource awareness, service awareness, and service constraints (such as the connection bandwidth and delay requirement between ECNs) and allocate them to multiple ECNs for collaborative computing. In addition, the CCF can open the resource and service information for the service fabrics through open interfaces so that the service fabrics can automatically control the scheduling process of the workload.

d. Data collaboration
ECNs adapt to the southbound multi-bus protocol. The east-west connections between ECNs use a unified data connection protocol. Through data collaboration, ECNs can exchange data and knowledge models with each other. The exchange modes include simple broadcast and Pub/Sub.

e. Multi-view display
Services can be displayed by tenant or service logic, shielding physical connection complexity. For example, each tenant only needs to view its own workload, distribution of the workload on the CCF, and resource usage.

f. Open service interfaces
The CCF provides workload requests, resource status feedback, and scheduling and execution status feedback through open interfaces to shield physical differences between smart assets, smart gateways, and smart systems.

Development Service Framework (Smart Service)

Figure 4.6: Function view: development service framework

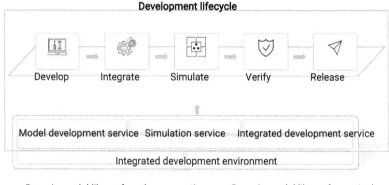

Domain model library for edge computing industries   Domain model library for vertical

The edge computing model library and vertical industry model library are integrated through the integrated development platform and tool chain to provide full-lifecycle services for the development, integration, simulation, verification, and release of models and apps.

The development service framework supports the following key services:

a. Model-based development service

•   Support model definitions including the architecture, function requirements, and interface requirements.

•   Support visualized display of the model and service processes.

•   Support generation of multi-language codes based on models.

•   Support integration and mapping of the edge computing domain models and vertical industry domain models.

•   Support model library version management.

b. Emulation service

•   Support software and hardware simulation of ECNs, allowing the specifications such as memory and storage space of ECNs to be simulated in the target application scenarios. The system needs to support fine-grained componentization and component tailoring and re-packaging (system reset) to match ECN specifications.

•   Based on simulation nodes, build networks and systems based on application scenarios, and perform low-cost and automated function verification on the developed models and apps in a simulation environment.

c. Integrated release service
•   Obtain the release version from the baseline library, invoke the deployment operation service, and deploy the models and apps to real ECNs.

Deployment Operation Service Framework (Smart Service)

The framework includes the following key services: service orchestration, app deployment (not prescribed in this document), and app market.

1) Service orchestration service
Generally, the service orchestration service is based on a three-layer architecture.

• Service orchestrator
The orchestrator defines service fabrics, which are generally deployed on the cloud (public or private cloud) or local systems (smart systems). The orchestrator provides a visualized workflow definition tool and supports Create/Retrieve/Update/Delete (CRUD) operations. The orchestrator can orchestrate services based on the service templates and policy templates defined by the development service framework and reuse the templates. Before delivering a service fabric to the policy controller, the orchestrator can perform semantic check and policy conflict detection on the workflow.

• Policy controller
To ensure real-time service scheduling and control, the policy controller is deployed at the network edge to implement local control.

Based on certain policies and the services and capabilities supported by the local CCFs, the policy controller allocates the service flows defined by a service fabric to a local CCF for scheduling and execution.

Because the edge computing domain and vertical industry domain require different domain knowledge and system implementation, the controller design and deployment are generally implemented by domain. The edge computing domain controller is responsible for deploying edge computing services such as security and data analysis. If the vertical industry service logic is involved, the vertical industry domain controller is responsible for distribution and scheduling.

• Policy executor
Each ECN has a built-in policy executor, which is responsible for translating policies into local device commands and performing local scheduling and execution. ECNs can either passively receive policies delivered by the controller or proactively request policies from the controller.

The policies need to focus only on high-level service requirements without implementing fine-grained control on ECNs. This ensures the autonomy of ECNs and real-time responses to local events.

2) App market service
The app market service connects consumers and suppliers, and can transform the unilateral

innovation of an enterprise into the multilateral open innovation in an industry ecosystem. Suppliers can encapsulate the industry know-how into apps and register them with the app market for quick publishing. Consumers can easily find an app matching their requirements from the app catalogue and subscribe to the app.

The app market service supports a wide range of apps, including the mechanism models constructed based on industrial knowledge, algorithm models constructed based on data analysis methods, service fabric models that can be inherited and reused, and apps that support specific functions (such as fault diagnosis). These apps can be directly used by end users or used for secondary development through model-based open interfaces.

Management Service

•   Support the unified management service oriented to terminals, network devices, servers, storage, data, isolation between services and apps, security, and distributed architecture.

•   Support the full-lifecycle management of engineering design, integration design, system deployment, service and data migration, integration testing, and integration verification and acceptance.

Full-Lifecycle Data Service

1) Edge data characteristics
Edge data is generated at the network edge and includes machine running data, environment data, and information system data. It features high throughput (large transient traffic), fast flow movement, diversity, strong correlation, and high requirements on real-time analysis and processing.

Compared with business big data scenarios such as Internet, smart analysis of edge data has the following characteristics and differences:

• Causal relationship vs. association relationship
Edge data is mainly targeted at smart assets that generally run with explicit input and output causal relationships, whereas business big data focuses on data association relationships.

• High reliability vs. low reliability
Industries such as manufacturing and transportation have high requirements on the accuracy and reliability of models. If the accuracy or reliability is low, property loss or even personal injury may occur. In contrast, business big data analysis generally has low requirements on reliability. It is required that the edge data analysis result be explainable. Therefore, black-box deep learning is restricted in some application scenarios. The combination of the traditional mechanism models and data analysis methods is the innovation and application direction of smart analysis.

• Small data vs. big data
Assets such as machine tools and vehicles are designed and manufactured by people. Most data in their running process is predictable, and only data generated in abnormal or critical conditions is truly valuable. On the other hand, business big data analysis requires mass data.

2) Full-lifecycle data service

Service fabrics are used to define the full-lifecycle data service logic, including specifying the data analysis algorithms. CCFs are used to optimize the data service deployment and running to meet real-time service requirements.

The full-lifecycle data service includes the following:

• Data pre-processing
Filter, clean, aggregate, and optimize (including dirty data elimination) raw data and perform semantic parsing.
•   Data analysis
•   Based on streaming data analysis, process data in real time so that events and ever-changing service conditions and requirements can be responded to quickly, accelerating the continuous analysis of data.
•   Provide the common statistical model library, and support the algorithm integration of models such as statistical models and mechanism models.
•   Support model training methods such as lightweight deep learning.
•   Data distribution and policy execution.

Execute policies locally based on predefined rules and data analysis results, or forward data to the cloud or other ECNs for processing.

• Data visualization and storage
Using technologies such as TSDB can significantly conserve storage space and meet the requirements on high-speed read and write operations. Next-generation interaction technologies such as AR and VR are used to provide a vivid display effect.

Security Service

The security design and implementation of the edge computing architecture are first expected to provide the following features:

•   Security functions adapt to the specific architecture of edge computing.
•   Security functions can be flexibly deployed and expanded.
•   The system can continuously mitigate attacks within a certain period of time.
•   The system can tolerate function failures to a certain extent and within a specified range, while basic functions run properly.
•   The entire system can quickly recover from failure.

In addition, the security design and implementation need to take the following unique features of edge computing scenarios into consideration:

•   Lightweight security functions can be deployed on IoT devices with limited hardware resources.
•   The traditional trust-based security model is no longer applicable to the access of a large number of heterogeneous devices. Therefore, the security model (such as the whitelist function) needs to be re-designed based on the minimum authorization principle.
•   Isolation between networks and domains is implemented on key nodes (such as smart gateways) to control the scope of security attacks and risks, preventing attacks on a node from spreading to the entire network.

- The security and real-time situation awareness functions are seamlessly embedded into the entire edge computing architecture to achieve continuous detection and response. Automation should be implemented as much as possible, but manual intervention is also required at times.

Security design must cover each layer of the edge computing architecture, and different layers require different security features. In addition, unified situation awareness, security management and orchestration, identity authentication and management, and security O&M are required to ensure maximum security and reliability of the entire architecture.

ECN security: Includes basic ECN security, endpoint security, software hardening and security configuration, secure and reliable remote upgrade, lightweight trusted computing, and hardware safety switch. Secure and reliable remote upgrade can fix vulnerabilities, and install patches in time, and prevent system failures after the upgrade. Lightweight trusted computing is applicable to simple IoT devices with limited computing (CPU) and storage resources to solve basic trust problems.

Network (fabric) security: Includes firewalls, IPS/IDS, anti-DDoS, VPN/TLS, and the reuse of security functions of some transport protocols, such as the REST protocol. Anti-DDoS is particularly important in IoT and edge computing. In recent years, a growing number of attacks on IoT devices are DDoS attacks. Attackers control IoT devices with poor security (such as cameras with fixed passwords) to attack specific targets.

Data security: Includes data encryption, data isolation and destruction, data anti-tampering, privacy protection (data anonymization), data access control, and data leakage prevention. Data encryption includes encryption during data transmission and storage. Data leakage prevention for edge computing is different from that of traditional systems because edge computing devices are usually deployed in distributed mode. Special considerations are required to ensure that data will not be leaked even if these devices are stolen.

Application security: Includes security functions such as whitelist, application security audit, malicious code prevention, web application firewall (WAF), and sandbox. The whitelist function is important in the edge computing architecture. The traditional trust-based security model is no longer applicable to the access of a large number of heterogeneous terminals and various services. Therefore, security models (such as the whitelist function) with minimal authorization are used to manage applications and access rights.

Security situation awareness and security management and orchestration: Since a large number of diversified terminals are connected at the network edge and services carried on the network are complex, passive security defencse is ineffective. Therefore, more proactive security defencse methods are required, including Big Data–based situation awareness, advanced threat detection, unified network-wide security policy execution, and proactive protection. These can facilitate quick responses. In combination with comprehensive O&M monitoring and emergency response mechanisms, maximum security, availability, and reliability of the edge computing architecture can be ensured.

Identity and authentication management: Covers all function layers. However, accessing a large number of devices at the network edge places much pressure on the performance of the traditional centralized security authentication system, especially when many devices go online within a short period of time. Therefore, the decentralized and distributed authentication and certificate management can be used if needed.

Deployment View

The edge computing architecture provides the following typical deployment models: three-layer model and four-layer model.

1) Three-layer deployment model

This model is applicable to scenarios where services are deployed in one or more scattered areas, each with a low traffic volume.

Typical scenarios include smart street lamps, smart elevators, and smart environmental protection.

After local processing of smart assets, multiple types are offered, multiple service data flows are aggregated on the smart gateways along the north-south direction. In addition to network functions such as supporting the access and local management of smart assets and bus protocol conversion, the smart gateways provide real-time streaming data analysis, security protection, and small-scale data storage. The gateways process real-time service requirements locally, and aggregate and send non-real-time data to the cloud for processing.

2) Four-layer deployment model

This model is applicable to scenarios where services are deployed centrally and the traffic volume is high.

Typical scenarios include smart video analysis, distributed grid, and smart manufacturing.

The typical differences between four-layer deployment and three-layer deployment are as follows: At the edge, there is a large amount of data and many local application systems are deployed. Therefore, a large amount of computing and storage resources are required. After the most real-time data processing is completed on smart assets and smart gateways, data is aggregated on local distributed smart systems for secondary processing. The distributed ECNs exchange data and knowledge through east-west connections, support horizontal elastic expansion of computing and storage resources, and implement real-time decision-making and optimization operations locally.

Chapter 12.
Edge Computing & IoT

IoT market analysts expect the edge to play a significant role in supporting IoT implementations going forward, as it creates efficiencies and scale in networks that makes IoT deployments more self-sustaining. IDC (International Data Corporation) estimates that that by 2020, IT spending on edge infrastructure will reach up to 18 per cent of the total spend on IoT infrastructure.[1] Mobile operators have the demonstrable capability to manage infrastructure, data and applications for IoT services, and are well placed to continue this with edge for IoT.

Rapidly increasing numbers of IoT devices and resultant data, mean that new techniques to meet customer requirements and ensure effective management need to be explored. Alternatives to the traditional IoT model of sending all data to the cloud for processing are required as the volume of data

to be processed explodes, and the cost of centrally storing and processing every piece of data, important or not, becomes harder to justify. This is particularly important for IoT services, as they can generate large volumes of new data for analysis. Edge computing is a deployment model which aims to push the relevant data processing and storage attributes closer to where the device is located. This means that data can be processed more efficiently, and many attri-butes do not need to be centralised. Mobile operators are well placed to enable edge computing to scale and enhance IoT deployments, additionally allowing options for data processing on behalf of customers to be further incorporated into their service offerings.

However, implementation of edge computing for IoT by mobile operators is not without challenges.
New investments, infrastructure and management platforms may be needed. Today, edge computing is a relatively immature technology that has been domi-nated by traditional cloud providers. Other members of the IoT ecosystem, including mobile operators, do have roles to play but as the IoT is still evolving, it will take some time for appropriate commercial and technical models to emerge.

This chapter explores the benefits to the IoT of edge computing and some of the different use cases where it could be applied. It explores the potential operator role for IoT edge computing and identifies some potential next steps to be undertaken by

the industry.

IoT reference model

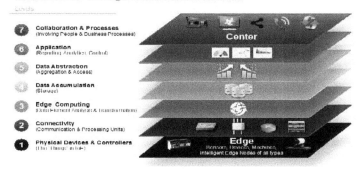

Internet of Things Reference Model

7 Collaboration & Processes
(Involving People & Business Processes)

6 Application
(Reporting, Analytics, Control)

5 Data Abstraction
(Aggregation & Access)

4 Data Accumulation
(Storage)

3 Edge Computing
(Data Element Analysis & Transformation)

2 Connectivity
(Communication & Processing Units)

1 Physical Devices & Controllers
(The Things in IoT)

Figure 12.1: IoT reference model (cisco 2014)

IOT reference model contains broadly seven layers. Researchers have a different opinions about thea number of reference layers; it varies from 3 to 7.

Physical Devices and Controllers

This layer has physical devices like sensors for sensing and assembling information about the surroundings which senses some physical parameters or identifies other smart objects in the environment.

Connectivity

In connectivity layer, communications, and processing are executed by existing networks. This layer includes connectors like RJ45, ModBus, USB or wireless connectivity.

Computing

The objective of computing layer is for mainly analyszing of data and data formation. Data is prepared by encoding, decoding, summarizing and transformation of data. This layer is also known as edge computing.

Data Accumulation

Data storage and data functionality are handled in this layer. This considers type of data, processing of data, higher level application data compatibility, combining of data and storage type. In the area of huge Data backend Hadoop, HBase, MongoDB, and Cassandra can be addeding for data storage.

157

Data Abstraction

The data abstraction layer receives data, sent from the devices stored at data accumulation layer and then sends to an endpoint to be used by the application. This sentence is not clear. The collected data is in many different formats as collected from different sources; it needs to be converted in the same format suitable forto a higher-level application. Data is indexed, normalized and provided withing appropriate authentication and authorization for security.

Application (Reporting, Analytics, Control)

The main objective of the application layer main objective is information interpretation and Software for interactions with previous data abstraction level. Simple communications applications can be handled like Mobile Applications are based on device data, business, programming patterns, and software stacks, operating systems, mobility, application servers, hypervisors, multi-threading, multi-tenancy, etc.

Collaboration and Processes (Involving people and business processes)

The information generated in IOT yields to accomplish in this layer by handover to end user and processes. They use applications and associated data for their specific requirements. Sixth layer Applications layer gives
the right data, at the right time, so they can do the right thing. People must be able to communicate and collaborate, sometimes using the traditional Internet, to make the IoT useful.

Mobile operators should view IoT edge computing as a flexible, distributed processing point beyond the core where network control, application logic, device management and data processing and analytics can be separated to enable a wide variety of deployment models along with automated and efficient management of IoT devices and data.

Location of the IoT edge from a mobile operator point of view

Key Benefits of Edge for the IoT

Edge for the IoT brings potential benefits for many IoT deployments, including decreased response time along with increased communications efficiency, compared to using the cloud to process and store data. For example, many IoT processes can have a high level of automa-tion at the edge resulting in low latency for rapid data processing. Only the most important information need then be sent to the cloud for further action or investigation.
Many new IoT services, such as intelligent vehicles, drones or smart grids, could come to rely on edge computing. Many of the benefits of IoT edge will need to be refined in proof of concept deployments by mobile operators to demonstrate that the model is beneficial. Benefits of IoT edge computing that have been identified include:

1. Low latency.
By its nature, the edge is closer to the IoT device than the core or cloud. This means a shorter round-trip for communications to reach local processing power, significantly speeding up data communica-tions and processing.

2. Longer battery life for IoT devices.
Being able to open communication channels for shorter periods of time due to improved latency, means that battery life of battery powered IoT devices could be extended. dDistributed ledger, or a hybrid open source ledger implementation such as BigchainDB could be used to obtain the advantage of a distributed ledger which provides features from the NoSQL database MongoDB on which it is based.

3. More efficient data management.
Processing data at the edge makes simple data quality management such as filtering and prioritisa- tion more efficient. Completing this data adminis-tration at the edge, means cleaner data sets can be presented to cloud based processing for further analytics.

4. Access to data analytics and AI.
Edge processing power and data storage could all be combined to enable analytics and AI, which require very fast response times or involve the processing of large 'real-time' data sets that are impractical to send to centralised systems.

5. Resilience.
The edge offers more possible communication paths than a centralised model. This distribution means that resilience of data communications is more assured. If there is a failure at the edge, other resources are available to provide continuous operation.

6. Scalability.

As processing is decentralised with the edge model, less load should ultimately be placed on the network. This means that scaling IoT devices should have less resource impact on the network, espe-cially if application and control planes are located at the edge alongside the data.

Unique Requirements of Edge for the IoT

IoT edge requirements are different to those from non-IoT edge computing use cases. The IoT needs to support a large number of devices, many of which do not have their own dedi-cated data processing resources, but that may be generating a large volume of data.

The relationship between these devices and the edge is different from that of other connected devices such as smartphones, where much of the data processing can be completed on the device. In non-IoT use cases, the edge is often used to serve constant volumes of data to the end device so that to enable services such as video streaming, or offer low latency applications for VR and gaming.

DIFFERENCES BETWEEN EDGE FOR IoT AND NON-IoT

For some customers, the IoT and other services will possibly share the same physical infrastructure and enablement platforms as non-IoT services. This means that considerations for the IoT need to be taken in the deployment of any edge infrastructure. If the IoT is to share edge resources with non-IoT services, then it may be necessary to have dedicated resources allocated on the edge node or gateway to support required levels of service. IoT services often run 24/7 while other edge use cases may only run intensively at peak times of day. Therefore, there needs to be consideration of the scope of IoT requirements on resources to ensure they can be met, even at peak times.

Use Case for IoT Edge
The following use cases have been identified as some of those which may be able to benefit from IoT edge computing to improve the level of service for IoT devices and applications.

IoT Foundation

Device Management

There are many device attributes and configurations that can be controlled at the edge, with many device management platforms extending their functionality to manage devices connected to edge infrastructure. Below are examples of four different attributes that device management at the edge will need to support:

Distributed firmware updates
The use of the edge gateway to distribute firmware updates locally, with distribution being managed by the edge node as opposed to the queuing system typically used when a firmware update is distributed centrally.

Device configuration updates

Devices at the edge will need to be configured locally as services change. The edge
    could be able to
manage this remotely.

Diagnostics of connected devices

The use of analytics at the edge can be used to identify specific problems with devices in the field through machine learning or pattern recognition.

Edge node or gateway management

Device management platforms can be used to manage the operator's edge infrastructure
    as well as the IoT
device.

Better control at the edge

Device management at the edge means that IoT devices are better controlled resulting in increased efficiency and improved quality of service. Where constraints are identified in edge computing, addi-tional resources can be brought online to reduce problematic areas and better manage service scalability. Additionally, IoT services such as data access by third parties can be managed effectively if control is available at the edge node.

Better management of device performance

Enforced consistency of device configurations and performance criteria at the edge mean that there are fewer variables to contend with, which means in turn, that applications can be confidently optimised to obtain best the best performance. Additionally, device performance data can be collected effec-tively at the edge for further analysis.

Effective deployment of applications at the edge

The use of a device management platform at the edge means that applications can be distributed to appropriate edge locations. If an IoT deployment has a number of different edges to manage, an application can be deployed to the edge closest to the device to obtain lowest latency, if a customer is paying for a premium service.

More efficient distribution of device updates

Distributing patches and firmware updates to devices is a key feature of a device management platform. Bringing edge infrastructure into the ecosystem means that these updates can be made more efficient as the edge can better manage local network resources for distribution to local devices.

Integrated hardware and software ecosystem

Device management that manages all aspects of the edge, including devices, applications and

connectivity means that a single ecosystem can be created, where control is able to be exerted across all elements of an edge deployment. This means that the service can be optimised for different uses, enhancing quality of service as a result.

Design Considerations for Device Management at the Edge

Device management at the edge allows efficiencies of IoT deployments to be fully realised. By reduc-ing the load on the cloud and its associated device management and analytics engines by moving processing to the edge, the system as a whole becomes more efficient.

Support for device types
The device ecosystem is very diverse and there-fore management of devices at the edge must be tailored to support different types, classes and configurations of IoT device. Some of these devices will have more computing power than others and the device management platform will have to understand which devices can operate indepen-dently and which will rely more heavily on edge processing or require centralised management in the cloud.

Context awareness
As IoT devices perform a wide range of functions at all times of day, the device

management services at the edge will have to be aware of the device context- this means not applying updates at a time when an IoT device might be especially active, or in certain locations.

▩Multi-access edge computing
Some edge devices will use multiple networks to communicate with the cloud (as per the ETSI Multi-access Edge Computing model2). This means that device management needs to be aware of which network a device is using and what data its being passed across it. This may affect configuration management if some updates can only be performed over certain networks.

Security

The IoT, by its very nature, is a distributed, complex network of devices. Edge computing pushes much of the logic and data storage for effective operation of the IoT closer to the end devices, and having security services also distributed at the edge offers the opportunity **to improve security capabilities, as well as offering native security for new low latency applications.**

The edge has an important role to play in data security. Many advanced tools and techniques can be applied to ensure that the edge contributes to the security of the overall IoT deployment. With a vast array of different equipment and devices connected to the IoT, security services at the edge can be used to comprehensively secure or even isolate complex industrial environments such as smart factories and buildings, as well as be used to ensure that data privacy is maintained in applica-tions handling personal data such as CCTV or automated licence plate readers.

Security at the IoT edge should be treated the same as any other secure environment, but there are new tools that can be used to ensure security at new edge and device levels. For example, using strong identity management for devices at the edge means that authentication is more straight-forward, as does robust definition of edge process-es to ensure that they remain secure.

A number of security issues can be addressed at the edge in an IoT environment:

▩Firmware and other updates
Secure update of firmware and other device updates from the edge using public key certifica -tion or secure transmissions such as SSL ensure that firmware upgrades are carried out securely.

▩Data Authentication
Authentication of data and updates at the edge is important to retain secure environments. Authenti-cation is likely to be via a certificate-based system. Implementation of this will need careful consid-eration to prevent poor performance of edge processing and latency.

▩Access Control
Identity and permissions management at the edge is important to ensure that access to data at the edge is managed securely. Granting data access to third parties means that full access control policies must be in place.

Prevention of Denial of Service attacks

Analysis of the data flow from IoT devices to spot and prevent characteristics of DDoS attacks.

Benefits of the Edge to this Use Case

The distributed nature of edge computing for IoT means that malicious attacks aimed at the network are harder to instigate as attacking single nodes will only have limited impacts. The edge also offers more processing power to prevent attacks such as DDoS in addition to the central core.

The IoT edge offers a new way of securing IoT end-points which may not be running the most up- to- date firmware or operating system. Security services at the edge can be used to ensure that devices with a high risk profile can be more easily isolated or have their data actively intercepted and secured.

Data and device provenance – as processing and data storage moves closer to the edge, then the origination point of data is better understood and can be recorded with greater confidence.

Processing of authentication, identity and access management – although sometimes constrained, additional processing power at the edge can be used for robust security processes as well as customer applications, meaning that security processes can be applied to ever increasing volumes of data.

Design Considerations

Using the edge environment to enhance IoT security could improve trust for the service being offered, but there are a number of considerations that should be considered in any deployment.

Constrained resources

Processing resources at the edge are constrained compared with centralised services, and so the same models for securing data and access at the edge may not be the most effective to apply at the edge – at the very least they will need to be re-configured to best make use of the resources available.

Appropriate policies

IoT at the edge must have relevant policies avail-able that are applicable to both IoT and edge use cases. These policies must be applied whenever data access is granted or updates are to be sent to devices. Failure to implement robust policies will mean that attacks are more likely to succeed.

Minimise attack vectors

By focusing IoT activity at the edge through, for example, only selective data generation and collec-tion, some attack vectors could be minimised. Holding and transporting less data makes both the system more secure, andbut also frees up system resources for better security management and authentication. The location of data processing needs to be appropriate – there may be classes of IoT data which can only be analysed in the cloud or highly secured data centres, for example.

Priority Messaging

Much of the data generated by the IoT will be of low value – unexceptional status updates and low priority data. However, some data will be of great importance and needs to be prioritised to ensure it is acted upon rapidly. This 'critical data' is likely to be a very small percentage of the total volume generated, yet is the most important. The scope of priority messaging goes beyond just single applications, as these message types could be used to initiate a cascade of actions across different applications and devices.

Examples of priority messaging include:

Transportation - accident alert that needs to be sent to following vehicles to enable them to avoid collision.

Health & Safety - fire alarm linked to building evacuation.

Environmental - rainfall or pollution above maximum safe levels linked to remedial activities.

Security – unauthorised activity leading to automated security actions e.g. doors clos-ing; terrorism response in immediate vicinity; drones flying into no-fly areas.

Industrial – failure of critical component requiringed immediate shutdown of other systems; construction worker in unsafe location.

The edge enables high priority data needs to be generated, sent, processed, and actioned more quickly than sending the data to the cloud.

Design Considerations

Fast processing at the edge – low latency means that priority messages can be acted upon more quickly at the edge. Having relevant data storage and applications in a local cloudlet means that messages are received and acted upon quickly, without having to rely on centrally held data or applications.

Message association – devices do not need to operate in isolation at the edge, and a priority message from one device may well be replicated by another nearby, meaning that the scale of any issue can be quickly judged.

Routing – processing of priority messages at the edge means that their routing can be optimised through the rest of the network architecture, so they get to a specific endpoint in the fastest possible time.

Battery life – - data prioritisation at the edge means that low powered IoT devices can save battery life and processing power by leaving the actioning of critical data to the edge node.

Design Considerations

Priority messaging will need to be considered as part of the overall design of IoT products, networks and data processing services. There are different types of priority messaging. Primarily, priority messages are in a known format as an output of a known process, for example, a fire alarm. Sometimes the message may not be identified as high priority by the device, but processing at the edge could still identify it as such. For example, voltage fluctua-tions in a smart grid may need the aggregation of data from different devices to determine priority.

High priority messaging and subsequent actions are enabled by the IoT edge. By only communi-cating with local IoT gateways and cloudlets, and keeping the impact of priority messaging local, faster responses can be assured. Data that has a wider impact beyond the immediate locale can be uploaded to the central cloud for further dissemi-nation and decision making either immediately or after the local situation has been handled;, for example, to feed in to larger datasets for analytics purposes.

For high priority messaging to be actioned quickly, near real-time processing of data is required. When tagged data is received, it can be easily identified and prioritised if the correct classifications are set-up within applications at the edge gateway. For other data, further processing could be used to identify data coming from multiple applications and devices to allow it to be prioritised in the same way.

The application on the edge node or gateway will need to make an automated decision as to what action to take with a high priority message. It may well be that a pre-defined process is initiated for known data types from known applications or devices. For example, a drone drifting into unau-thorised areas can be redirected to a new flight path through a pre-defined process that all drones will need to recognise.

" By only communicating with local IoT gateways and cloudlets, and "keeping the impact of priority messaging local, faster responses can be assured."

Data Replication

Many IoT services are not localised – they are spread across a large geographic area or devices need to move between different locations on the mobile network. To support low latency at the edge, some applications may need access to a localised data store at each location that they move to. This data store needs to be consistent across all instances of the application to ensure consistent results. This data may be time sensitive – a weather forecast, traffic conditions or distributed ledger instance, for example. Without access to this data locally, applications will need to query the cloud, which will affect latency and creates single points of dependency. By replicating data across multiple sites, this issue can be avoided, and a seamless experience created at every location.

Benefits of Edge for this

Use Case

Replicated data has the following benefits:

- Efficiencies of IoT at the edge can be fully realised, across multiple locations. Not having to call to the cloud for master data significantly increases the performance of an application.

- Low latency support – by having local direct access to relevant data at the edge, low latency can be better realised.

- Disaster recovery - by distributing data across multiple locations, disaster recovery becomes possible, as data can be replicated across multiple locations, reducing the risk of data loss even if a node were to fail.

◌Scalability - heavy processing of data can be distributed across all available processing power, meaning that a system is not reliant on a single cloud or core source for transactional processing power. Distribution may be possible across different vendor systems with the correct standards in place.

Design Considerations for Replicated Data

There will generally be a need to have certain data ultimately held in the cloud for long-term storage, analytics and future processing. However, real-time data and logic that is needed for the operation of a wide variety of services under an IoT edge comput-ing architecture must be available as an application needs it, without the latency implicit in storing and processing data centrally.

◌Time synchronisation

In order to synchronise data replicated across multiple locations, there will likely need to be time synchronisation at all edge locations. To ensure consistent data across multiple nodes, time must be accurate, otherwise data at different locations may not be fully synchronised.

◌Preventing task duplication

The use of distributed ledgers to store transactions at edge nodes is a good way to ensure consistency of data and messages across replicated nodes – once a message or task has been completed, this could be recorded in the ledger to ensure that the activity is replicated to every peer node.

◌Master data

Although distributed data is important for real-time transactions, a master data set is likely to be need-ed from a central location, to govern how the local instances should operate. Centralised operation of multiple cloudlets is needed to ensure that there is a distinct hierarchy in place for issue resolution and effective control of multiple systems.

◌Personal data

As data is replicated across nodes, special consid-eration should be given to personal data that would be affected by the EU GDPR and similar regula-tions. Data replication processes should have scope to identify personal data and the way that should be handled.

◌Node to node communication

If enabled, nodes are able to communicate with each other. This means that a process of ensuring that data sets are replicated without reference to master data sources inside the cloud. Data must be replicated directly into other nodes where the local application may need access to up- to- date data.

◌Security

Data authentication at the edge requires local attributes to be held to ensure data is authenti-cated with low latency. Holding this information in the centralised cloud would slow down operations where authentication is needed.

Device management

Device configurations may need to be replicated across multiple nodes at the edge to ensure that any device management services are applied at the appropriate time or location.

Cloud Enablement

The edge is expected to be attractive to cloud vendors as it offers them the potential to better distribute data storage and processing power to support low latency services, support higher systems availability and also to reduce the load on their existing data centres. A mutually beneficial relationship between cloud providers and mobile operators should exist at the edge, where operators have local resources to enable IoT edge for cloud providers, and cloud providers have platforms suitable for enabling a wide range of services on the operator's edge infrastructure. Local infrastructure also meets customer and regulatory requirements about data storage on premises or in the country, if edge resources can be located in the relevant location. Some IoT users such as factories or smart cities may also insist on their data being stored and managed locally.

From a service point of view, IoT edge environ-ments will rarely operate completely in isolation. A connection to a centralised cloud will often be required for control, monitoring and update purposes at the very least, and so the dynamic between the edge and cloud is a complex one. A hybrid edge and cloud architecture can offer the best of both worlds.

Built-in scalability

By enabling distributed resources, scalability of IoT services at the larger end of the scale becomes

achievable. Even if resources at the edge are unable to cope with the scale of operations required by a deployment, there can be a fallback to the cloud, meaning that some or all of the service can be maintained.

Benefits of Edge for this

Use Case

Linking the IoT edge and cloud has many benefits, across network, application and data management.

Maximise use of resources both locally and centrally

By linking the edge and the cloud, the most appropriate resources for specific tasks 167 can be identified and allocated. This means efficient usage of resources in the operators domain, perhaps held at local base stations, or on the device itself, or in the cloud providers domain, where huge data volumes can be centrally stored.

▢ Integrated view of data

Integrating the edge and cloud means that users will have a view over the status and location of all data relevant to their application or service. A seamless view means that the quality of service which can be achieved without having to resort.

▢ Security

Full integration of edge and cloud means that data security can be overseen from a single source. Utilising the relevant cloud agents ensures that data can be securely transmitted across the cloud, edge and device.

▢ Enablement of new business models

Business models including Infrastructure as a Service (IaaS) or higher response level Service Level Agreements enabled by lower latency can be introduced with integrated cloud and edge access. Unified billing for processing and storage can be managed across the cloud and edge in processes seamless to the end user. The edge can reside in different locations of the IoT deployment chain, and any cost benefits can be used to create new busi-ness models.

Design Considerations

▢Approach to data processing

A "Slow Lane" / "Fast Lane" approach is necessary to ensure that data is held in the correct location and processing resources are prioritised accord-ingly. "Fast Lane" data will obviously be dealt with first, and likely to be processed as fully at the edge as possible, for all the reasons stated elsewhere in this paper. "Slow Lane" data on the other hand is likely to be backhauled at an appropriate time to the cloud for processing. "Slow Lane" data may provide a more comprehensive view of what is occurring, but it will take time to achieve that view. To facilitate this model, appropriate data analytics models and data categorisation need to be put into place by the analytics provider.

▢Support for cloud agents

Many cloud providers have dedicated edge agents that will manage the relationship between the edge and the cloud. Recognition of these and integra-tion of support for them into wider application and device management platforms will enable cloud integration for a wide range of service providers and encourage portability of applications.

▯Developer support

Developers commonly look to incorporate cloud support and functionality in their applications, and the same will be true of IoT applications at the edge. Access to the edge infrastructure and platforms should be implemented in the relevant tools to enable the developer community to take advantage of benefits edge offers the IoT.

"Integrating the edge and cloud means that users will have a view over "the status and location of all data relevant to their application or service."

IoT Solutions

IoT Image and Audio Processing

Devices such as cameras, including CCTV, and microphones can provide data for processing by IoT platforms and applications, such as licence plate reading or monitoring noise pollution. IoT edge introduces new ways of analysing this data without having to backhaul the entire image or audio stream. An edge cloudlet can be used to process the image, video or audio data to determine key information, such as licence plate numbers or the number of people in an area, meaning that only a small amount of data, such as the licence number

itself is forwarded or stored. Other examples where the camera can be used as a sensor include for monitoring of environmental conditions such as river levels, monitoring crowd density, or in industrial IoT, whether on a factory floor, monitoring powerlines from a drone, or listening for flow through pipelines to identify leaks.

Benefits of Edge for this Use Case

▯Low cost

Cameras and microphones are relatively low cost to procure, install and maintain for the insights they can provide; use of edge processing means that network management costs are also managed effectively, making them an attractive general purpose alternative to dedicated IoT sensors.

▯Significant reduction in network backhaul

By identifying objects within images, without needing to send the image itself to upstream servers, the amount of data that needs to be transmitted back to the core is significantly reduced.

169

Quick decision making

Fast processing means that it is possible to support a wider range of real-time or near real-time appli-cations – speeding up the management of produc-tion lines or enabling new ways of charging drivers at tollgates and so on.

More flexible IoT sensor arrays

By adding camera data to IoT deployments, a more comprehensive analysis can be taken, as cameras can add more general context (through both imag-ing of a location and broad image coverage) than many other types of IoT sensors.

Enabling new use cases

New IoT use cases become possible with the use of cameras and microphones as sensors. For example, the use of image processing for recognising yields, pests and diseases of crops whilst they grow.

Design Considerations

Design and deployment considerations for image and audio processing mainly focus on image and camera setup to ensure that the data source is good enough for analysis, but other considerations are also relevant.

Image or audio quality

Information can only be recognised from a camera image or audio stream if the quality is good enough

– this means high enough resolution, but also the ability to recognise from an image or audio stream in all environmental conditions – day and night, sun and rain, crowd/ traffic. If this is not possible, the analytics will not be fit for purpose.

Image & audio format

Images can be still or video and along with audio can come in a variety of formats and obtained using a variety of standard and proprietary proto-cols. Analytics engines will need the image data to be decoded to frame data. Video images may need to be broken down into a series of still images for analysis. Collected data will ideally be in a common, open format so that its can be managed by a range of analytics engines.

Data analytics

A picture is worth a thousand words, but for IoT analytics purposes, there needs to be a very clear definition of the parameters that are needed from an image or audio file, so that machine learning processes can be trained. This means that a clear definition of the image topography or audio land-scape and how it relates to the data to be extracted must be defined in advance.

Camera setup

In some cases, it may be simpler if the camera is in a fixed position with a number of reference points that do not change, so that the image process-ing engine can accurately identify the area of the image to process.

Operator Opportunity

IoT Foundation

The edge is a natural evolution of today's IoT architecture deployed by mobile operators. Evolution of plat-forms, processes and propositions will enable operators to introduce edge seamlessly into their foundational IoT services, such as connectivity and device management, whilst retaining the attributes which they are renowned for – connectivity, security and scalability.

The edge offers new ways of creating efficient connectivity services specifically designed to benefit IoT deployments by reducing the amount of data which is backhauled to the cloud. Better options for managing devices in the field become available, with distributed management of firmware updates and applications possible. IoT platforms will need to extend their reach to the edge, and operators will be in a strong position to ensure that network, security and cloud services are integrated effectively at the edge.

IoT Service Enablers

Data Management at the edge will be crucial for operators in ensuring quality of service and effec-tive analytics of IoT data. Managing customer data in a secure fashion and ensuring a seamless integration between user, cloud, application, edge and device will allow a new generation of service offerings from operators.

IoT devices can benefit greatly from local process-ing power, data management and analytics. Having the ability to prioritise messages and manage the large volume of data from massive IoT deploy-ments means that operators can both maximise

the cost savings on their own network, but pass on better service levels to their customers.

There is a mutually beneficial relationship with cloud providers that operators can also build, through a combination of local infrastructure controlled by the operator, and the data manage-ment platforms from cloud providers, to enable a new generation of IoT management services.

IoT Solutions

The edge offers operators both opportunities for new IoT solutions, and new ways of managing existing services. IoT sensors which generate large amounts of data such as cameras can be used

to provide new or better insights, and data from multiple sensors can be combined to create new levels of analysis.

Advanced IoT solutions such as support for V2X communications or smart factories can benefit from these new opportunities that operators can introduce. By making the edge the standard place for managing applications and services, new levels of service management, automation and precision can be achieved.

Potential Next Steps

Deployment of IoT edge and applications that will utilise it is not a trivial task, and there are a number of chal-lenges that will need to be addressed. Operators will need to strike a balance between the benefits that edge brings in scaling and managing IoT deployments and the costs of setting up a service. A number of potential next steps for the industry have been identified:

Common Framework

⬜Define end user requirements for customers ⬜and application developers.

⬜Define where the IoT edge resides for defined ⬜use cases – at the cloudlet in the data centre, on the base station, or closer to the device.

⬜Understand deployment and business models ⬜and match to the infrastructure that could be utilised.

Evaluate Solutions

⬜Evaluate different edge models, consortiums⬜ and technologies for their suitability to IoT deployments.

⬜Understand the need for IoT platform ⬜extensions at the edge, and how the functionality available maps to IoT use cases.

Operator Roles

⬜Understand the roles of different partners ⬜through the value chain and how the operator can create value for them.

⬜Understand cloud offerings at the edge and ⬜how the operator can integrate with them

or support them. Engage with cloud providers to create a mutually beneficial model for deployment of edge services from both the operators and cloud providers.

Undertake relevant pilots and other activities to investigate the benefits of edge for

IoT customers.

Chapter 13.
Standards and Role of open source

This chapter describes the standardization/open source activities required to support the previously identified needed services and capabilities.

Standards for self-organization, self-configuration, self-discovery

There is no doubt that with the growth in the number of ECNs, the management of the network, the ECN and the application will become a huge challenge. To facilitate the deployment of ECNs, it is better to mask the complexity of the technology from operators and users, and to realize the plug and play of devices. Therefore, it is necessary to introduce autonomic networking. Currently, the autonomous functions already exist. However, the discovery, node identification, negotiation, transport, messaging and security mechanisms, as well as non-autonomic management interfaces, are being realized separately. This isolation of functions is leading to high OpEx.

Engineering Task Force (IETF) is developing a system of autonomic functions to manage the network at a higher level without detailed low-level management of individual devices. In a secure closed-loop interaction mechanism, the network elements cooperate to satisfy management intent: network processes coordinate their decisions and translate them into local actions.

In the cellular communication domain, 3GPP has proposed the self-organizing network (SON), aimed at making the planning, configuration, management, optimization and healing of mobile radio access networks simpler and faster. Since Release 8, 3GPP has begun the research and standardization of SON, the motivation being to deal with more parameters in network configuration, more complex network structures and the coexistence of the 2G/3G/LTE network. Newly added base stations should be self-configured to realize the plug and play. Moreover, based on network performance and radio conditions, the base station will self-optimize its parameters and behaviour. When outage occurs, the self-healing will be triggered to temporarily compensate the performance loss before a permanent solution is found.

Standards which allow low OpEX management of ECN and software will also be self organized as well.

Trust/ decentralized trust

The ISO/IEC 15408 Standard defines trust as "a calculation configuration in which components, operations or processes involved in the calculation are predictable under any condition and are resistant to viruses and physical disturbances".

Trust in this sense means that the services provided by the computer system can be proved to be trustworthy. In other words, the services provided are trustworthy from the user's point of view and this trustworthiness is provable.

Trust computing as defined by the Trust Computing Group (TCG) has the following meaning:

§ User authentication: the trust of the user
§ Platform hardware and software configuration ⬛correctness: the user's trust in the platform environment
§ The integrity and legitimacy of the application: ⬛the trust in the application running
§ Verifiability between platforms: the mutual ⬛trust between the platforms in the network

The decentralization trend is driven by the distributed system;, for instance, an edge computing system, in which no central hub acts, so a new approach to security and trust are needed based on the distributed architecture.

There exists a general view that the blockchain's distributed architecture offers a valid framework for tackling distributed system security and trust challenges. The blockchain is a distributed database that maintains a continuously growing list of records, called blocks, secured from tampering and revision. Each block contains a timestamp and a link to a previous block. By design, blockchains are inherently resistant to modification of the data – once recorded, the data in a block cannot be altered retroactively.

ISO Technical Committee 307 is now dedicated to standardization of blockchains and distributed ledger technologies to support secure and trust interoperability and data interchange among users, applications and systems.

Credible information

Credible information is crucial for an edge computing system. Credibility of information depends on trust in the system which generates the information. Trust is defined to be "confidence that an operation, data transaction source, network or software process can be relied upon to behave as expected" in IEC 62443-3-3 [63]. IEC 62443-3-3 describes system security requirements for industrial automation and control systems (IACS), and it currently does not list trust as a requirement explicitly. Even though security implies a guarantee of trust, it can be useful to review whether some additional system requirements, e.g. requirements on system integration and operation, are necessary to realize trust in IACS. It can also be beneficial to investigate what additional requirements are necessary when dealing with trust in horizontal edge computing systems.

E/W communication Standards between multiple ECNs

There are several layers of E/W communication in question:

1)   Physical layer: Aa number of Standards exist for mesh networking via physical layer relay and any of these can/could be used. It might be worth considering how that mesh might be implemented efficiently in wired networks, and also whether the physical radio Standards might be merged with the narrowband IoT protocols for long-range operation.

2)   Link layer protocols: hHere again, numerous protocols exist (IEEE 802.1aq in wired, and IEEE 802.15.4-ZigBee [64] or Z-Wave [65] and WIA-PA in wireless). Again, a merge with narrowband IoT protocols should be considered to allow mesh operation in narrowband IoT for long range operation.

3)   In the autonomous control domain, time-sensitive data must be

transmitted within strict bounds of latency and reliability. In the case that E/W-bound communication is required between ECNs in industrial automation, automotive or robotic environments, TSN may be needed to prioritize time-sensitive traffic in crowded networks. TSN is currently under development within IEEE 802.1 and the Deterministic Networking working group of IETF.

4)   Data layer: Aa flexible data ontology, allowing common definition of data types and meanings across the network. This is an area where both Standards bodies and open source may play a role, such as one M2M and OPC-UA.

The majority of open source work might be concentrated in the area of high level data processing in the mesh by elaborating on existing, proven and recommended Standards (such as MQTT) within an open reference architecture. For example, an overarching reference architecture could employ a lightweight MQTT implementation to accept not only north/south (N/S) but also E/W transactions between modules. This could be implemented as a single queue (all transactions E/W, N/S) or as two queues, one operating for E/W and another for N/S. It can be noted that in the items above, a mesh can be implemented at each layer, but it is only with the inclusion of item 3) that an application level E/W communication can be achieved.

Finally, a successful implementation of E/W communication depends on implementation of decentralized trust.

Containerization Standard for embedded systems

Linux containers, Docker for example, offer for the first time a practical path to using virtualization on embedded devices, as the latter do not require a very complex hypervisor architecture to operate. Containerization of IoT applications, particularly at the ECN level, would be greatly facilitated by the creation of a common Standard for virtualisation support on IoT nodes. This would be an expansion of the ground covered by OCI [60], which has initiated a general effort.

There are a number of challenges facing an implementation:

§ The extreme heterogeneity of device type
§ Severely restricted resource envelopes in ▨terms of storage, CPU, and networking
§ Devices that are difficult to reach or re-provision upon failure, where power is unstable and may be turned off at any time, or which have custom hardware attached, requiring deep version interoperability,. i.e. when the device returns online after weeks or months, an upgrade to the container can be made spanning several versions.

Open standard for implementation of algorithm for machine learning

As discussed earlier, the complexity of CNNs, HMMs, natural language processing and other disciplines used in the creation of ML algorithms and DNNs requires storage and computing resources. Clearly the backend processing in embedded devices is currently an open source initiative, and since it has started in this manner, it is likely to remain so, with Caffe and a few others becoming de facto Standards.

To implement ML upon lower powered, cheaper, embedded devices, it would seem to be a reasonable approach to implement a specific hardware-based method of accepting the introduced ML models and then acting upon them, i.e. comparing the models with incoming live data.

Already some efforts have been made in this area;, for example, the recent Intel Quark implementation of comparison functions [59]. These efforts are proprietary and no Standards have been defined to cover the loading and comparison of features.

If Standards were defined in the loading of models and comparison of data, it would provide the greatest degree of interoperability between different offerings from different processor manufacturers.

Comprehensive standard tackling carrier mode selection in case of loss of connectivity
Connectivity is offered by many providers of mobile andbut also Wi-Fi networks. Some even have global coverage or globally scattered coverage;,
178

for example, iPass, a network of Wi-Fi access points across the globe, or Eduroam that has Wi-Fi access points across universities.

Currently, human users can select the network and input the credentials. Some locations, e.g. hotels, offer a QR code for the credentials.

In the case that the connection is lost, the human has to intervene and connect to a new network. For IoT or safety and security use cases, this interaction is not possible or even productive. There are Standards for sending recommendations regarding which networks to use, with associated policies;, for example, Open Mobile Alliance (OMA) Device Management, based on HTTP. The Standard was adopted by 3GPP on the interface between the UE and the ANDSF network component. It supports recommended network policies depending on the time of the day, the location and the prioritized networks to be connected. The UE can thus connect independently to a new network when connectivity is lost. Unfortunately, the policy does not include the very important aspect of price. Being a Standard oriented to the telecommunications industry, it did not reach out to the outside community.

For tackling IoT use cases, OMA has defined a new protocol, OMA Lightweight M2M that uses a more energy-efficient transport based on UDP. Its connectivity management policies are developing and it might have a broader impact on providing connectivity without human interaction.

Even so, there is a tremendous need across the vertical sectors to have a comprehensive standard tackling carrier mode selection, according to the connectivity modules built on the end device, be it Wi-Fi, 3G, LTE, soon 5G or any other type of access network.

Role of open source

Cloud computing has immensely benefitted from open sources such as Linux, Docker containers, Kafka messaging, Spark streaming and multi-tier storage. The result has been a highly scalable and standardized infrastructure that meets computational and lifecycle management demands and provides a common environment for developers, driving down the cost of software solutions.

179

The need for standardization and open source for the edge is even greater. The edge is where vendor-specific solutions need to interoperate. Without this interoperation, IoT cannot fulfil its promises.

As discussed earlier, microservices or pods need to be deployed on the edge (devices, IoT gateways, micro data centre, etc.) as well as in the cloud, so that applications can be configured in an optimal way, e.g. to address huge data volumes, real-time requirements and variances in connectivity.

As history has shown, open source projects fulfil these needs better than standardization of interfaces and architectures.

Companies providing solutions in edge computing will have plenty of room for differentiation and revenue generation by providing differentiating functionalities, domain specific solutions, better services, higher QoS, etc.

At the time of the writing of this White Paper, the Linux Foundation project Edge X Foundry appears to be a candidate to address a common edge computing platform.

Chapter 14.
Introduction to Edge Computing in IIoT

Almost every use case and every connected device focused on by the Industrial Internet Consortium (IIC) requires some sort of compute capability at its source, at the edge. Multiple sources define edge computing as "cloud computing systems that perform data processing at the edge of the network, near the source of the data". While this is certainly true, it only scratches the surface of the immense power and remarkable capabilities that edge computing applications and architectures can provide to solve industrial internet users' toughest challenges. But, as is typical with any powerful technology, innovative architectures and new terminology are needed to facilitate implementation, bringing increased complexity with it.

This chapter provides practical guidance on edge computing, architectures and the building blocks necessary for an edge computing implementation. It defines edge computing architectural functions and highlights key use case considerations.

Consequently, there is a need to identify:
- where the edge is,
- its defining characteristics,
- key drivers for implementing edge computing and
- why compute capabilities should be deployed at the edge in Industrial Internet of Things (IIoT) systems.

It also informs architecture and testbed teams through:
- identifying and evaluating standards, practices and characteristics best suited for addressing edge computing holistically, and highlighting gaps where needed,
- identifying deployment models and crosscutting functions that address patterns and characteristics for edge computing deployment and
- exploring and identifying extensions to the current edge computing model that expand and enhance the functionality of edge computing devices.

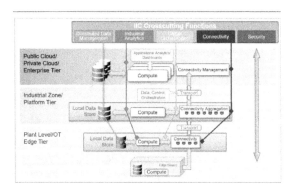

Figure 14.1: IIoT Architectures

Where is the Edge?

The edge is a logical layer rather than a specific physical divide, so it is open to individual opinion and interpretation of "where" the edge is. The business and usage viewpoints provide clues, while the functional and implementation viewpoints deal with the technical aspects.

From the business perspective, the location of the edge depends on the business problem or "key objectives" to be addressed.

"Key objectives are quantifiable high-level technical and ultimately business Quote outcomes expected of the resultant system..." and "Fundamental capabilities refer to high-level specifications of the essential ability of the system to complete specific major business tasks". (Ref IIRA).

There is a continuum of fundamental capabilities for an IIoT solution and "the edge" moves along this continuum based on the requirements of the problem at hand, as shown by the following examples found in typical industrial operations.

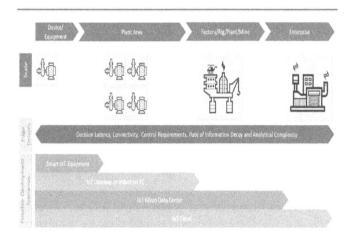

Figure 14.2: Edge Layers

EXAMPLE 1: MONITOR THE PERFORMANCE OF PLANT AREAS OR PRODUCTION LINES

The performance of equipment and production lines are often expressed through performance indicators like Overall Equipment Effectiveness (OEE). Near real-time analytics on multiple data points from sensors in the plant area can be processed on a local gateway and provide OEE trends and alerts to operational systems or personnel. In this case, the fundamental capability requires information from multiple equipment sources to perform simple analytics. The time value of information is high as response delays waiting for decisions from the cloud can cause significant losses. This business problem suggests that the edge is at the plant area level.

EXAMPLE 2: OPTIMIZE SUPPLY CHAIN FOR A LOCATION OR FACTORY TWICE DAILY

Optimizing supply chain processes for a local facility, factory or an oil field requires data from multiple sources at short intervals to apply optimization algorithms and analytics that will adapt supply-chain plans in business systems such as SCM or ERP. The fundamental capability requires local or factory-level connectivity with decisions made in hours. Additional

183

information outside the perimeter of the factory may be useful, but not mandatory for effective optimization. In this instance, the edge is at the perimeter of the factory, plant or local facility.

EXAMPLE 3: PREDICT EQUIPMENT FAILURE AND SCHEDULE PROACTIVE RESPONSE

Machine learning models to predict Electric Submersible Pump (ESP) failures require data from multiple offshore platforms. The analytics models are complex and a large amount of data is needed to train and re-train the models. It also requires regular data feeds from operating ESPs to determine each unit's remaining useful life. The data from individual ESPs need to be analyszed regularly but information decay is much slower than in the other scenarios and decisions can be taken daily or weekly. Computation is typically performed at the enterprise level using a public or private cloud and is at the top end of the edge continuum.

The edge can be anywhere along the time-value graph (see Figure 7.3) as these examples illustrate.

It is "where" data for sensors is used to achieve a specific key objective or address a specific business problem.

Why Compute at the Edge

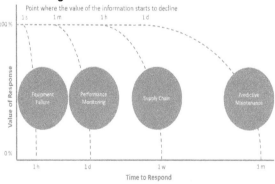

Figure 14.3: Time-Value Graph

Edge computing is a decentralized computing infrastructure in which computing resources and application services can be distributed along the communication path from the data source to the cloud. That is, computational needs can be satisfied "at the edge," where the data is collected, or where the user performs certain actions. The benefits are:

- improved performance,
- compliance, data privacy and data security concerns are satisfied and
- reduced operational cost.

We examine each in turn.

IMPROVE PERFORMANCE

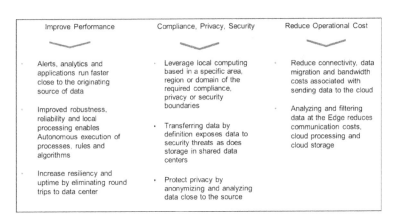

Improve Performance	Compliance, Privacy, Security	Reduce Operational Cost
Alerts, analytics and applications run faster close to the originating source of data	Leverage local computing based in a specific area, region or domain of the required compliance, privacy or security boundaries	Reduce connectivity, data migration and bandwidth costs associated with sending data to the cloud
Improved robustness, reliability and local processing enables Autonomous execution of processes, rules and algorithms	Transferring data by definition exposes data to security threats as does storage in shared data centers	Analyzing and filtering data at the Edge reduces communication costs, cloud processing and cloud storage
Increase resiliency and uptime by eliminating round trips to data center	Protect privacy by anonymizing and analyzing data close to the source	

The edge is not merely a way to collect data for transmission to the cloud, it also processes, analyszes and acts on the collected data at the edge within milliseconds and is therefore essential for optimizing industrial data at every aspect of an operation.

In a windfarm, for example, if wind speed or direction changes, the edge software onsite can analyzse this data in real-time and adjust individual turbines to optimize overall wind farm production. Only aggregated data is sent to the cloud, reducing communication bandwidth requirements and improving data transfer time.

In addition, the turbines generate terabytes of data. Sending this data to a cloud platform to run advanced analytics may be technologically achievable, but cost prohibitive to do daily. Through edge computing, the end user can capture streaming data from a turbine and use it in real-time to prevent unplanned downtime and extend the life of the equipment while reducing the data set to a more manageable size for transmission to the cloud.

The challenge of transmitting large quantities of data in real-time cost-effectively from remote industrial sites can be mitigated by adding intelligence to devices at the edge of the network, in the plant or field. Edge computing on the device brings analytics capabilities closer to the machine and provides a less expensive option for optimizing asset performance.

COMPLIANCE, DATA PRIVACY AND DATA SECURITY

Public cloud creates a long list of privacy, regulatory and compliance issues related to classified or sensitive data. Today, service providers can guarantee private access and control but at the price of being cumbersome, costly, inelastic and difficult to manage.

Edge computing allows enterprises to operate independently using a public/private cloud by using local computing based in that area, region, domain or the required local security boundaries.

REDUCE OPERATIONAL COST

Connectivity, data migration, bandwidth and latency features of cloud computing are expensive. Edge computing addresses these by reducing bandwidth requirements and latency.

If an oil and gas company drilling in Nigeria, for example, requires computing to predict oil-well production-decline rate, the alternatives are to build their own data centrers (with the associated cost and scale limitations) or to use a cloud provider (where the nearest datacentrer can be 5,000 miles away) with significant costs and unreliable service. With edge computing, the end user can process data in real time locally at a fraction of the cost of the public cloud, while still maintaining the flexibility that a cloud infrastructure provides.

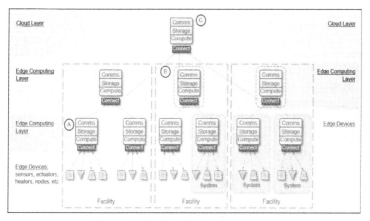

Figure 14.4: Cloud Infrastructure

Edge computing creates a valuable continuum from the device to the cloud to handle the massive amounts of data generated from IIoT. Processing data closer to where it is produced and at the response times required by the local applications addresses the challenges of rapidly increasing data volume. Edge computing decreases response time to events by eliminating a round trip to the cloud for analysis. It avoids costly bandwidth additions by eliminating the need to transmit gigabytes of data to the cloud. It also protects sensitive IIoT data by analyszing it locally within a private network.

Consequently, enterprises using edge computing may improve and optimize operational performance, and address compliance and security concerns while efficiently managing costs.

The examples progress from left to right as the edge layer becomes more complex and aggregates multiple system functions below. The computing layer moves up the architecture stack, aggregating processing capabilities, information and data from below.

The multitude of choices means there is a layered edge-cloud synergy, rather edge versus cloud. Where possible, digitalization is always going to use edge and cloud synergistically in which fast and localized compute take

187

place at the edge while global compute, model development, management and security can benefit from the "wisdom of the cloud".

Starting with an example of a simple temperature controller, the problem to be solved is temperature monitoring and control of a specific device or zone. In this case, the edge devices would be the thermocouple sending temperature data and the element providing the heating or cooling, and the edge computing device would be the temperature controller running the control algorithm and making the adjustments.

If the objective is to orchestrate temperature across several devices or areas, then the edge becomes the temperature controllers themselves (whether individual components or standalone systems) and the edge-computing layer becomes the system coordinating the control, typically a
PLC or SCADA system ("B" in Figure 5).

If the business objective is to monitor and manage multiple geographically dispersed facilities, then the edge is each individual facility reporting its status to a compute layer in the cloud ("C" in Figure 5).

Characteristics of the IIoT Edge Computing Model

Edge computing exists vertically within the full stack from device to cloud and horizontally across IIoT subsystems. The new computing model is fully distributed and can support a wide range of interactions and communication paradigms including:

- peer-to-peer networking;, for example, security cameras communicating about objects within their scope,
- edge-device collaboration such as self-organizing vehicles that travel together or a community of wind turbines in remote locations,
- distributed queries across data stored in devices, in the cloud and anywhere in between,
- distributed data management, defining where and what data is to be stored, and for how long and
- data governance including quality, discovery, usability, privacy and security aspects of data.

Key Drivers: Cloud to Edge Computing

IIoT disrupts the cloud-computing model with new usage scenarios leading to these requirements:

Time sensitive: Often decisions need to be made within milliseconds while a round trip to the cloud introduces undesirable latency. Reliability and critical-path control management make it too risky to rely solely on remote logic. A good example is autonomous guided vehicles; although an anti-collision algorithm can execute in the cloud, it is best to run the algorithms at the edge.

Communication: Mobile network infrastructure tends to follow the pattern of deploying to highly populated urban areas, before trickling down to rural or remote locations. For assets that are truly remote, satellite connectivity may be the only option. This creates a paradigm where IIoT use cases for industries such as mining, oil & gas, chemicals and shipping are not well served by robust affordable communication.

Data boundary: In some applications, the data produced and consumed by devices is required by other devices only within the local area. This local data can be acquired and served with low latency by the edge to the users in the local area. Depending upon the use case, the radius of the local area can vary from a few centimetrers from the device to an entire neighbourhood or city. In augmented-reality scenarios, for example in smart cities, local edge infrastructures can store information about points of interest of a neighbourhood. Since most of the access to the data (or consumption of the data) will be made in the same local area, there is no need to store all information in the cloud. As a truck transitions from private to public network and across sovereign boundaries, both enterprise policies and local data regulation will determine what can be stored locally and what can be sent to the cloud.

Data volume: The amount of data generated by sensors can be huge. For example, hundreds of high-resolution cameras creating video streams at 30 frames per second could clog communication channels. Edge computing allows data to be processed and stored locally with only pre-processed data being transferred to the cloud.

IT/OT convergence: Historically the operational technologies (OT) that are used to manage and automate industrial equipment exist at the edge of the network while information technologies (IT) have been more centralized. Though these systems have been treated separately, there is value in having an integrated IT/OT strategy that offers:

•   business data needed for interpreting or contextualizing IoT data for decision making,
•   availability of both existing and new business outcomes, business models that leverage integrated data and
•   standard processes to drive outcomes.

Data governance deals with quality, discovery, usability, privacy and security aspects of data. Insufficient data governance can leave a company vulnerable to major business disruptions. On the other hand, extreme data governance can stifle innovation. Edge computing helps simplify data governance by:

•   reducing data clutter: high volume time-series data can be analyszed at the edge,
•   refining data usability: edge computing allows data to be contextualized resulting in better usability,
•   improving data privacy: security policy at the edge allows only relevant data shared with the systems up in the hierarchy and
•   lowering the impact of security breach: since edge computing allows for the data storage and analysis to be federated, impact of a security breach can be contained.

Use Cases

This section describes use cases that illustrate the benefits of edge computing. Figure 6 shows logical entities residing on either the cloud or the edge, connected through WANs. When clouds were first introduced, the trend was to "shift everything into the cloud", but, due to network latency and the cost to transmit a large amount of data, more logical tasks remained at the edge. With the improvement of the processing power and capability, the amount of tasks performed on the edge will continue to grow.

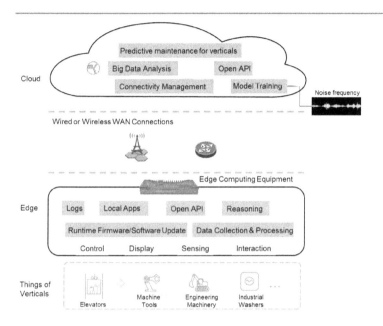

Figure 7.5: Logical Architecture Diagram for Edge Computing

To facilitate discussions on the boundaries and the necessary means to enable edge computing, there are "Key Requirements", "Edge Boundary" and "Edge Devices" clauses added to each use case. "Key Requirements" are not intended to be a standard so they are not normative. The "Edge Boundary" is one view from the contributor to the uses case and is not intended to be definitive as typically, the boundary of each service or application varies as drawn by the system designers.

Similarly, the term "Boundary Devices" portrayed in the use cases by the contributors is not an exhaustive list.

Through the examination of all the use cases described here, we inferred general requirements for edge computing that may be common to all use cases:

Communications: Edge devices must continue to function even though data communications may be temporarily interrupted.

191

Edge device capability: The edge devices need to support edge-computing capabilities: communication, local computing and local storage.

Edge device functionality: The edge devices can be customized with features to fit various vertical industries, such as compact size, low power consumption, anti-vibration, electromagnetic shielding, waterproof and dust proof.

CREW SAFETY MANAGEMENT

Objective: Use wearable multi-gas detectors to monitor employees' exposure to harmful gases during a shift. Create real-time exposure profiles using data from the sensors and adjust the work schedule or work flow to prevent health issues.

Description of the use case: Safety in a hazardous or life-threatening operating environment, such as a mine, is a top issue. Other issues are production related, such as the status of the tools used, the status of the conveyer or vehicles used to carry out the ore, and the amount of ore produced in a measured period.

Key Requirements:

1.   (Environment monitoring) poisonous gas detection, ambient temperature detection and control and lighting control need to be implemented.

2.   (Personal monitoring) the personal vital-sign monitoring system must be installed locally and the data sent out to a central monitoring station in the operation centrer.

Edge Boundary: Operation site (e.g. at the mine operation office or operation centrer).

Edge Devices: Personal vital sign monitor (body temperature, heart rate and blood pressure, CO_2 level), personal tracker, environment monitors (ambient temperature, CO level, hazardous gas detection, lighting), tools, trucks and unmanned vehicles, conveyer belts and weighting devices.

FLEET TRACKING AND PLATOONING

Objective: Combine real-time GPS data with vehicle usage data from sensors to monitor and optimize the location and status of the fleet.

Description of the use case: A trucking company must operate its vehicles safely and efficiently. In addition to optimal routing in the delivery routes, the mechanical status of each vehicle can contribute to timely maintenance to improve the operation efficiency and safety. The operation is originally designed for individual trucks, but it can be extended to several trucks to form a
"platoon" of unmanned trucks to increase operational efficiency.

Platooning is typically used for self-driving vehicles. The lead vehicle detects the lane and traffic condition to decide the optimal speed to maneuvermanoeuvre. This information is then communicated through the following vehicles in the platoon. Each car has vehicle-to-vehicle (V2V) communication capabilities and controls for driving safety. The lead vehicle gathers the information, such as the location of the fleet and the operating condition of each vehicle, and reports to the office.

Key Requirements:

1.   GPS based vehicle tracking supported by a local map.

2.   The vehicle status monitoring system is installed locally, and the data shall be sent out to a central monitoring station in the operation centrer.

3.   A connection to a central location providing traffic updates

Edge Boundary: The lead vehicle of the platoon.

Edge Devices: Vehicle status monitor (engine speed, temperature, break pad thickness and hydraulic subsystem, transmission subsystem, weight and shock status, tire pressure, fuel level, etc.), GPS tracker, environment monitors (ambient temperature, lane detection, vicinity vehicle detection), container status monitor (for refrigerating) and V2V driving safety devices.

PREDICTIVE MAINTENANCE-CONNECTED ELEVATORS

Objective: With edge applications installed on connected elevators, operators and technicians are able to perform predictive maintenance of the elevators based on the data they provide at the edge.

Description of the use case: Operators of connected elevators rely on edge functions to achieve predictive maintenance of their systems for the systems to become more reliable and reduce system downtime. The operational cost of these systems is greatly reduced since the efficiency of the system can be significantly improved.

A connected elevator uses many sensors for gathering data on noise, vibration, temperature, etc. The operational status of the elevator can then be derived from analyzsing the sensed data. With elevators connected to edge computing devices, and the sensed data uploaded to the cloud, elevator operators can obtain the running status of all of their elevators. Elevator technicians are then able to perform predictive maintenance using edge computing data, and data in the cloud, to check and maintain those elevators selectively that are more likely to fail based upon analytics. Predictive maintenance increases the operational efficiency of the equipment while reducing the maintenance expense through targeted failure prevention and avoidance of unplanned downtime.

Key Requirements:

1.   The edge devices offer containers, open APIs that allow third parties to develop applications to be installed on the edge devices.

2.   To support 7 x 24 monitoring, the edge devices support runtime update of its software and firmware.

Edge Boundary: The elevator operations centrer or the elevator itself

Edge Devices: Infrared sensors, weight sensors, smoke detectors, vibration inductors, noise sensors, cameras and operator interfaces.

Objective: Regulations in the food industry (e.g., EC 128/2002) require manufacturers to establish systems that enable traceability of food products across all stages of production, processing and distribution. While this use case focuses on the food industry, product traceability is important across multiple industries.

Description of the use case: Pieces of plastic in chocolate bars, bacterial contamination of cream cheese, falsely declared ingredients in pasta-based ready meals—a food product may be recalled for any number of reasons. Time is of the essence when it comes to product recalls. As well as damaging the manufacturer's reputation, these situations can be expensive, with costs rising as the whereabouts of the end products become less clear.

Bar codes, 2D codes, or electronic transponders are used to identify objects depending on whether they are individual items, primary and secondary packaging, pallets, trucks or containers. When it comes to deciding which technology to use, financial factors and the objects and processes involved must be taken into account. For example, a bar code can be printed onto an egg, while the cartons holding six or twelve eggs can be labelled with 2D codes and additional plain text such as the best-before date. A transponder, on the other hand, can be added to shipping cartons, pallets and other aggregated containers. The various methods of product identification described above ensure that the flow of materials across the supply chain are labelled, identified and tracked.

Industrial machinery, automated guided vehicles (AGVs) and collaborative robots or "cobots" are increasingly prevalent on the factory floor. The most targeted applications are packaging and palletizing, pick and place, machine tending and assembly and quality inspection. As issues may occur at any step in the supply chain including the quality or handling of materials, contamination introduced by people or machines or faulty processes, product quality and product traceability require orchestrating, recording and verifying the people, processes and machines involved.

Sensors with edge-computing capabilities allow these product identification methods to be checked against stored data for verification to ensure the flow of goods, people, process and machines. The right product goes into the right package and onto the shelf with critical information appearing correctly on the package and full genealogy available in the cloud.

Key Requirements:

1. Consider ambient conditions when selecting edge devices within the food industry, such as humidity, cold storage and outdoors.

2. Location and tracking of items across all stages of production, processing and distribution is important.

3. Sensors and computer vision systems identify particulates or contaminants in food.

4. Sensors and edge computing to orchestrate, record and verify the people, processes and machines involved.

Edge Computing and Industrial Analytics

Analytics is broadly defined as a discipline transforming data into information and business value through systematic analysis. Industrial analytics is the use of analytics in IIoT systems.

Advanced analytics is at the core of this next-generation level of transformation and, when applied to machine, process and grid data, provides new insights and intelligence to optimize decision-making and enable intelligent operations leading to transformational business outcomes and social value. These new insights and intelligence can be applied across any level of any industry if the appropriate data can be collected and analytics applied correctly. Some say data is the new oil. If that's the case, then data analytics is the new engine that propels the IIoT transformation.

Analytics can be classified in a number of different ways depending on where they are performed, the window of time for a relevant and meaningful response, and what functionality they are trying to achieve. A single analytical flow could involve edge analytics for initial distillation of data and immediate actuation, analytics in the cloud comingling the latest news from the edge with historic big data stores and back to the edge for further actuation.

TECHNOLOGY AND THE EVOLUTION OF INDUSTRIAL ANALYTICS

Advances in IT and OT capabilities such as compute capacity, communication bandwidth, low latency, software capability and sensor technology have removed technological constraints and allowed analytics to be deployed through an entire IoT system. For instance, looking at the edge tier of a system, the processing capability available at the edge in conjunction with low-latency communication have enabled algorithms to be run in real time supporting models that generate insights and real-time control for the system. Similarly, looking at the cloud tier, what was once impractical, performing streaming analytics on enormous data sets, is now possible thanks to big data compute capabilities and high-bandwidth communications. These same advances have also enabled the distribution of analytics so that they need not be centralized and can be implemented across the IIoT ecosystem.

WHERE SHOULD THE ANALYTICS BE PERFORMED?

Most industrial analytics deployments use a hybrid approach where analytics run at all tiers from edge to cloud, with analytics at a particular tier addressing a specific business objective.

Cost benefits stem from reducing the amount of data being sent to and stored in the cloud. Edge analytics mitigates the cost of storing and processing low-value and oft-repeated data. Analytical models are not helped by data noise. Instead of creating an unnecessary noisy big data problem, edge analytics can distill data prior to sending it on to the cloud.

Security Considerations for Edge Computing

Security is an important consideration for edge computing. More components and communication channels create a greater potential for attack vectors. Innovations are required to monitor, manage and secure globally distributed systems and contain inevitable breaches. The IISF documents a generalized end-to-end security framework. In edge computing implementations:

- security must be built-in to each device and at every level of the architecture,

- computing and networking endpoints must be monitored and

managed,

- latest patches must be applied,

- attacks must be isolated and quarantined and

- affected components must be able to be healed.

Orchestration

The centralized nature of cloud computing enables access to a scalable and elastic pool of shareable physical or virtual resources. As computing is distributed to the edge, resources can still be shareable, but elasticity is challenged because:

- compute resources could be in separate islands where they cannot communicate to coordinate computation,

- locations of compute resources may be difficult or costly to access,

- compute in ruggedized enclosures might not be expandable and

- technicians to perform the work may not be easily available at the edge.

With these limitations, the approach is inverted. Understanding both the "as-built" compute target and net-available resources is critical to deploying the right software to the right location. Once deployed, tools to manage, monitor and secure the entire lifecycle are required. Software may need to be throttled or redeployed, memory usage restricted, databases and logs truncated if resource thresholds are challenged. We also need to predict usage trends to address issues before they occur.

The challenge for developers and administrators is to understand not only the physical requirements of their applications (computing inputs, outputs, connectivity, etc.), but also the security and processing requirements and how those requirements translate to different CPU and OS types. Industry standard calculations and metrics may be required.

The two main activities essential to deliver an orchestration solution are:

- infrastructure management to handle the lifecycle of devices at the edge including the commissioning and provisioning of resources and

Introduction to Edge Computing in IIoT

- orchestration to manage the lifecycle of services and applications and the dependencies between them.

Various standardization efforts share this understanding of orchestration, such as the ETSI Multi-Access Edge Computing (MEC) initiative, the ETSI NFV Management and Orchestration (MANO).

Orchestration and infrastructure management at the edge poses challenges not faced in the cloud mainly due to:

Heterogeneity of devices and application domains: At the edge, there are no expectations on homogeneity regarding devices, or the hardware and software platforms. An infrastructure management system needs to be flexible enough to manage a plethora of devices to consume their resources seamlessly. To provide some level of homogeneity at the edge, both virtualization and containerization technologies may be employed. Also, devices can behave differently based on the application domain. An orchestration solution in a smart factory environment where the nodes are static and the network reliable will have a different behaviour from those orchestrating a logistics or smart cities domain where vehicles are consistently mobile and subjected to variable connection quality.

Different connectivity and communication technologies: IIoT gateways must handle multiple connectivity solutions using different protocols. The orchestrator must be aware of the available solutions to guarantee communication between deployed functions and applications.

Differences in capabilities, requirements and constraints: The higher level of homogeneity and the virtually infinite availability of resources in the cloud ease the orchestration process. Conversely, a broader range of service requirements, device capabilities and constraints are observed at the edge. For example, devices at the edge have different sensors, actuators, real-time operating system or networks;, some nodes can provide accelerators, others will not. The orchestrator must be aware of the capabilities found in the infrastructure. Also, the constraints on these nodes need to be known beforehand (e.g. bandwidth, battery, CPU power, memory). At orchestration time, a service must be able to describe its requirements, and the requirements will be checked against the available capabilities and constraints found in the infrastructure.

With that in mind, orchestrators can operate both vertically and horizontally. Vertical orchestrators handle services in a specific domain, while horizontal orchestrators manage services across different domains providing integration among them. An example would be a smart factory that relies on a logistics company, and each has its own orchestrator. A horizontal orchestrator composes services that span the different domains (e.g. a service that adjusts throughput of a production line based on the current location of the necessary supplies).

Orchestration is an important aspect of edge computing to provide a platform to support both IT and OT activities in IIoT. The ability to coordinate the deployment of new services and applications gives the edge the capacity to be programmable and deliver the services required by its consumers. While trying to ensure the quality of the service required, its presence in edge solutions needs to be enforced.

References

Ericsson, *Hyperscale cloud – reimagining data centres from hardware to applications*, May 2016 [Online]. Available: http://www.ericsson.com/res/docs/whitepapers/wp-hyperscale-cloud.pdf. [Accessed 19 September 2017].

SATYANARAYANAN, M., *The Emergence of Edge Computing*, IEE Computer, Vol. 50, pp. 30–39, January 2017.

International Data Corporation, *IDC FutureScape: Worldwide Internet of Things 2017 Predictions*, November 2016 [Online]. Available: https://www.idc.com/getdoc.jsp?containerId=US40755816. [Accessed 19 September 2017].

SIMSEK, M. et al., *5G-Enabled Tactile Internet*, IEEE Journal on Selected Areas in Communications, Vol. 34 (No. 3), March 2016.

ITU-T, *The Tactile Internet*, International Telecommunication Union, August 2014.

IEC, *Factory of the Future*, White Paper, 2017 [Online]. Available: http://www.iec.ch/whitepaper/ futurefactory. [Accessed 19 September 2017].

Mitsubishi Electric, *e-F@ctory*, 2017 [Online]. Available: http://sg.mitsubishielectric.com/fa/en/ download_files/solutions/e_Factory.pdf. [Accessed 19 September 2017].

PLAN.ONE, *PLAT.One Platform*, 2017 [Online]. Available: https://www.sap.com/products/iot-platform-cloud.html. [Accessed 19 September 2017].

5G-PPP, *5G Automotive Vision,* October 2015 [Online]. Available: https://5g-ppp.eu/wp-content/ uploads/2014/02/5G-PPP-White-Paper-on-Automotive-Vertical-Sectors.pdf. [Accessed 19 September 2017].

European Commission, *European strategy on Cooperative Intelligent Transport Systems (C-ITS),*

30 November 2016 [Online]. Available: https://ec.europa.eu/transport/themes/its/c-its_en. [Accessed 19 September 2017].

European Commission, *5G for Europe: An Action Plan,* 14 September 2016 [Online]. Available: ec.europa.eu/newsroom/dae/document.cfm?doc_id=17131. [Accessed 19 September 2017].

IEEE 802.11p-2010, *IEEE Standard for Information technology – Local and metropolitan area networks – Specific requirements – Part 11: Wireless LAN Medium Access Control (MAC) and Physical Layer (PHY) Specifications, Amendment 6: Wireless Access in Vehicular Environments.*
15 July 2010 [Online]. Available: https://standards.ieee.org/findstds/standard/802.11p-2010.html. [Accessed 19 September 2017].

DOKIC, J., MÜLLER, B., MEYER, G., *European Roadmap: Smart Systems for Automated Driving,*

European Technology Platform on Smart Systems Integration (EPoSS), April 2015, [Online]. Available: http://www.smart-systems-integration.org/public/documents/publications/EPoSS%20 Roadmap_Smart%20Systems%20for%20Automated%20Driving_V2_A pril%202015.pdf. [Accessed 19 September 2017].

[14] *Dedicated Short-Range Communications (DSRC) Fact Sheet,* Intelligent Transport Systems Joint Program Office, U.S. Department of Transportation [Online]. Available: http://www.its.dot.gov/ factsheets/pdf/JPO-034_DSRC.pdf. [Accessed 19 September 2017].

5G Americas, *V2X Cellular Solutions,* October 2016 [Online]. Available: http://www.5gamericas.org/ files/2914/7769/1296/5GA_V2X_Report_FINAL_for_upload.pdf. [Accessed 19 September 2017].

BEDO, J-S., CALVANESE STRINATI, E., CASTELLVI, S., CHERIF, T., FRASCOLLA, V., HAERICK, W., KORTHALS, I., LAZARO, O., SUTEDJO, E., USATORRE, L., WOLLSCHLAEGER, M., *5G and the Factories of the Future*. 5G-PPP White Paper, 2015 [Online]. Available: https://5g-ppp.eu/wp-content/uploads/2014/02/5G-PPP-White-Paper-on-Factories-of-the-Future-Vertical-Sector.pdf. [Accessed 19 September 2017].

KOTT, A., SWAMI, A., WEST, B. J., *The Internet of Battle Things*, IEEE Computer, vol. 49, p. 70-75, December 2016.

Proximity-based services (ProSe); Stage 2, TR 23.303 3GPP; December 2016 [Online]. Available: https://portal.3gpp.org/desktopmodules/Specifications/Specification Details.aspx?specificationId= [Accessed 19 September 2017].

GOODYEAR, M., LOUIS, J.H., *Defining the Security Domain,* University of Kansas, 2015 [Online]. Available: http://slideplayer.com/slide/2353814. [Accessed 19 September 2017].

5G-Ensure, *5G Security Architecture* [Online]. Available: http://www.5gensure.eu/5g-ensure-architecture. [Accessed 19 September 2017].

Global Platform, *Internet of Things White Paper*, May 2014 [Online]. Available: https://www.globalplatform. org/documents/whitepapers/IoT_public_whitepaper_v1.0.pdf. [Accessed 19 September 2017].

ANCUTA CORICI, A., EMMELMANN, M., LUO, J., SHRESTHA, R., CORICI, M., MAGEDANZ, T., *IoT inter-security domain trust transfer and service dispatch solution*, 2016 IEEE 3rd World Forum on Internet of Things (WF-IoT), December 2016.

TAPSCOTT, D., TAPSCOTT, A., *Blockchain Revolution: How the Technology Behind Bitcoin Is Changing Money, Business, and the World*, Portfolio, Penguin Random House, New York, 2016.

SWAN, M., *Blockchain: Blueprint for a new economy*, O'Reilly Media, Sebastopol, California, 2015.

SZABO, N., *The Idea of Smart Contracts*, [Online]. Available: http://www.fon.hum.uva.nl/rob/ Courses/InformationInSpeech/CDROM/Literature/LOTwinterschool20 06/szabo.best.vwh.net/idea. html. [Accessed 19 September 2017].

SWANSON, T., *Consensus-as-a-service: a brief report on the emergence of permissioned, distributed ledger systems*, 6 April 2015 [Online]. Available: http://www.ofnumbers.com/wp-content/ uploads/2015/04/Permissioned-distributed-ledgers.pdf. [Accessed 19 September 2017].

ANTONOPOULOS, A.M., *Mastering Bitcoin: Unlocking Digital Cryptocurrencies*, O'Reilly Media, Sebastopol, California, 2015.

SIGNORIN, M., *Towards an internet of trust: issues and solutions for identification and authentication in the internet of things*, University Pompeu Fabra, Barcelona, Spain, 2015.

IBM, *Empowering the edge: Practical insights on a decentralized Internet of Things*. April 2015 [Online]. Available: https://www-935.ibm.com/services/multimedia /GBE03662USEN.pdf. [Accessed September 2017].

GOTTHOLD, K., ECKERT, D., *Deutschland erkennt Bitcoin als "privates Geld.* Welt N24 16, August 2013 [Online]. Available: https://www.welt.de/finanzen/geldanlage/ article119086297/Deutschland-erkennt-Bitcoin-als-privates-Geld-an.html. [Accessed 19 September 2017].

PETERS, M., *Software-Defined Storage: A Buzzword Worth Examining*, 18 January 2013 NetworkComputing.com [Online]. Available: http://www.networkcomputing.com/ storage/software-defined-storage-buzzword-worth-examining/1334995080

[IoT] Ovidiu Vermesan & Peter Fress, "Internet of Things –From Research and Innovation to Market Deployment", River Publishers Series in Communication, ISBN: 87-93102-94-1, 2014.

[SusAgri] Rodriguez de la Concepcion, A.; Stefanelli, R.; Trinchero, D. "Adaptive wireless sensor networks for high-definition monitoring in sustainable agriculture", Wireless Sensors and Sensor Networks (WiSNet), 2014

[sixlo] IETF WG 6Lo: http://datatracker.ietf.org/wg/6lo/charter/

[sixlowpan]   IETF   WG   6LoWPAN: http://datatracker.ietf.org/wg/6lowpan/charter/

[IANA-IPV6-SPEC] IANA IPv6 Special-Purpose Address Registry: http://www.iana.org/ assignments/iana-ipv6-special-registry/

[IEEE802.15.4] IEEE Computer Society, "IEEE Std. 802.15.4-2003", October 2003

[RFC2460] S. Deering, R. Hinden, "Internet Protocol, Version 6 (IPv6) Specification", December 1998, RFC 2460, Draft Standard

[RFC3315] Droms, R., Bound, J., Volz, B., Lemon, T., Perkins, C., and M. Carney, "Dynamic Host Configuration Protocol for IPv6 (DHCPv6)", July 2003

[RFC4193] R. Hinden, B. Haberman, "Unique Local IPv6 Unicast Addresses", RFC4193, October 2005

[RFC4291] R. Hinden, S. Deering, "IP Version 6 Addressing Architecture", RFC 4291, February 2006

[RFC4862] S. Thomson, T. Narten, T. Jinmei, "IPv6 Stateless Address Autoconfiguration", September 2007

[RFC6775] Z. Shelby, Ed., S. Chakrabarti, E. Nordmark, C. Bormann, "Neighbor Discovery Optimization for IPv6 over Low-Power Wireless Personal Area Networks (6LoWPANs)", November 2012, RFC 6775, Proposed Standard

205

[RFC6890] M. Cotton, L. Vegoda, R. Bonica, Ed., B. Haberman, "Special-Purpose IP Address Registries", RFC 6890 / BCP 153, April 2013

[roll] roll IETF WG: http://datatracker.ietf.org/wg/roll/charter

[I802154r] L. Frenzel, "What's The Difference Between IEEE 802.15.4 And ZigBee Wireless?" [Online] Available: http://electronicdesign.com/what-s-difference-between/what-s-difference-between-ieee-802154-and-zigbee-wireless.

BIBLIOGRAPHY:

A

ABC News, "100 million dieters, $20 billion: The weight-loss industry by the numbers," May 8, 2012.

ABI Research, Internet of Things vs. Internet of Everything: What's the difference?

May 7, 2014.

Adshead, Anthony, "Data set to grow 10-fold by 2020 as internet of things takes off," ComputerWeekly.com, April 9, 2014.

Alliance for Aviation Across America, "Air traffic modernization."

B

Bradley, Joseph, Joel Barbier, and Doug Handler, Embracing the internet of everything to capture your share of $14.4 trillion, Cisco, 2013.

Brynjolfsson, Erik and Lorin M. Hitt, "Beyond the productivity paradox," Communications of the ACM, volume 41, issue 8, August 1998.

Brynjolfsson, Erik, Lorin Hitt, and Heekyung Kim, "Strength in numbers: How does data-driven decisionmaking affect firm performance?" Social Science Review Network, April 2011.

Bughin, Jacques, Michael Chui, and James Manyika, "Ten IT-enabled business trends for the decade ahead," McKinsey Quarterly, May 2013.

C

Caterpillar Global Mining, "Automation keeping underground workers safe at LKAB Malmberget Mine," Viewpoint: Perspectives on Modern Mining, issue 3, 2008.

Chui, Michael, Markus Löffler, and Roger Roberts, "The Internet of Things," McKinsey Quarterly, March 2010.

City of Chicago, Office of the City Clerk, 2015 budget overview, 2015.

Consumer Electronics Association, "Record-breaking year ahead: CEA reports industry revenues to reach all-time high of $223.2 billion in 2015," press release, January 6, 2015.

D

Deutsche Bank, The Internet of Things: Not quite the Jetsons yet, but places to look,

May 6, 2014.

E

Eaton Corporation, Blackout tracker annual report for 2013, March 31, 2014.

The Economist Intelligence Unit, The Internet of Things business index: a quiet revolution gathers pace, October 29, 2013.

Evans, Peter C., and Marco Annunziata, Industrial Internet: Pushing the boundaries of minds and machines, General Electric, November 26, 2012.

F

Federal Trade Commission, Internet of Things: Privacy & security in a connected world, FTC staff report, January 2015.

G

Gartner Inc., Forecast: The Internet of Things, Worldwide 2013, December 2013.

Gartner, "Gartner says 4.9 billion connected 'things' will be in use in 2015," press release, November 11, 2014.

General Aviation Manufacturers Association, 2014 general aviation statistical databook & 2015 industry outlook, 2014.

Goldman Sachs, The Internet of Things: Making sense of the next mega-trend, September 3, 2014.

H

Henderson, Catherine, Martin Knapp, José-Luis Fernández, Jennifer Beecham, Shashivadan P. Hirani, Martin Cartwright, et al., "Cost effectiveness of telehealth for patients with long term conditions (Whole Systems Demonstrator telehealth questionnaire study): Nested economic evaluation in a pragmatic, cluster randomised controlled trial," The BMJ, volume 346, issue 7902, March 2013.

I

Identity Theft Resource Center, Identity Theft Resource Center breach report hits record high in 2014, January 12, 2015.

International Data Corporation, Worldwide Internet of Things spending by industry sector 2014–2018 forecast, July 2014.

K

Kwatra, Sameer, and Chiara Essig, The promise and potential of comprehensive commercial building retrofit programs, American Council for an Energy-Efficient Economy, May 2014.

L

Lomax, Tim, David Schrank, Shawn Turner, and Richard Margiotta, Selecting travel reliability measures, Texas Transportation Institute, Texas A&M University, May 2003.

Lopez Research, Building smarter manufacturing with the Internet of Things (IoT), part two, January 2014.

M

Matheson, Rob, "Moneyball for business," MIT News, November 14, 2014.

McKinsey & Company, Industry 4.0: How to navigate digitization of the manufacturing sector, April 2015.

McKinsey Global Institute, Big data: The next frontier for innovation, competition, and productivity, May 2011.

McKinsey Global Institute, Disruptive technologies: Advances that will transform life, business, and the global economy, May 2013.

McKinsey Global Institute, Infrastructure productivity: How to save $1 trillion a year, January 2013.

McKinsey Global Institute, Internet matters: The Net's sweeping impact on growth, jobs, and prosperity, May 2011.

McKinsey Global Institute, Open data: Unlocking innovation and performance with liquid information, October 2013.

McKinsey Global Institute, Urban world: Cities and the rise of the consuming class, June 2012.

McKinsey Global Institute, McKinsey Center for Government, and McKinsey Business Technology Office, Open data: Unlocking innovation and performance with liquid information, October 2013.

Merchant, Brian, "With a trillion sensors, the Internet of Things would be the 'biggest business in the history of electronics,'" Motherboard.vice.com, October 29, 2013.

Miller, Stephen, Base salary rise of 3% forecast for 2015, Society for Human Resource Management, July 9, 2014.

Morgan Stanley, The "Internet of Things" is now: Connecting the real economy, April 3, 2014.

Morgan Stanley, Wearable devices: The "Internet of Things" becomes personal, November 19, 2014.

N

New York City Department of Health and Mental Hygiene, New York City trends in air pollution and its health consequences, September 26, 2013.

New York State Department of Transportation, State fiscal year 2012–13 annual report, bridge management and inspection programs.

Nichols, Chris, "How the Internet of Things is changing banking," Center State Bank blog, September 16, 2014.

O

O'Donnell, Erin, "Cheating the reaper," Harvard Magazine, March–April, 2013.

P

Piore, Adam, "Designing a Happier Workplace," Discover, March 2014.

Porter, Michael E. and James E. Heppelmann, "How smart, connected products are transforming competition," Harvard Business Review, November 2014.

R

Ray, Tiffany, "Fitness spending still fast despite economy," The Press-Enterprise, July 6, 2012.

Rio Tinto, 2014 annual report: Delivering sustainable shareholder returns, 2015.

S

Salas, Maribel, M., Dyfrig Hughes, Alvaro Zuluaga, Kawitha Vardeva, and Maximilian Lebmeier, "Costs of medication nonadherence in patients with diabetes mellitus: A systematic review and critical analysis of the literature," Value in Health, volume 12, number 6, November 2009.

Schwartz, Tony, "Relax! You'll be more productive," The New York Times, February 9, 2013.

Scroxton, Alex, "How the internet of things could transform Britain's railways," ComputerWeekly.com, August 2014.

Sofge, Eric, "Google's A.I. is training itself to count calories in food photos," Popular Science, May 29, 2015.

Sullivan, Bob, and Hugh Thompson, "Brain, interrupted," The New York Times, May 3, 2013.

Synapse Energy Economics, 2013 carbon dioxide price forecast, November 2013.

T

Teu, Alex, "Cloud storage is eating the world alive," TechCrunch, August 20, 2014.

Tweed, Katherine, "Entergy tests AMI voltage optimization," Greentech Media, January 27, 2012.

U

Ubl, Stephen J., "Public policy implications for using remote monitoring technology to treat diabetes," Journal of Diabetes Science and Technology, volume 1, number 3, May 2007.

UK Department for Business Innovation & Skills, The smart city market: Opportunities for the UK, BIS research paper number 136, October 9, 2013.

UK National Institute for Cardiovascular Outcomes Research, National heart failure audit, April 2012–March 2013, November 2013.

United Nations Department of Economic and Social Affairs, World urbanization prospects, the 2014 revision, 2014.

US Bureau of Labor Statistics, American time use survey 2013, June 2014.

US Central Intelligence Agency, The world factbook.

US Department of Health and Human Services, Patient Provider Telehealth

Network: Using telehealth to improve chronic disease management, June 2012.

US Department of Transportation, National Highway Traffic Safety Administration, Traffic Safety Facts 2012, 2012.

US Energy Information Administration, Electric power sales, revenue, and energy efficiency Form EIA-861 detailed data files, February 19, 2015.

V

Van Marle, Gavin, "How 'augmented reality eyewear' can give you a smarter view of future logistics," The Loadstar, November 26, 2014.

Varian, Hal, "Kaizen, that continuous improvement strategy, finds its ideal environment," New York Times, February 8, 2007.

Vrijhoef, Ruben, and Lauri Koskela, "The four roles of supply chain management in construction," European Journal of Purchasing and Supply Management, volume 6, number 3, January 2000.

W

Weber, Lauren, "Go ahead, hit the snooze button," The Wall Street Journal, January 23, 2013.

Wilson, Marianne, "Study: Shrink costs U.S. retailers $42 billion; employee theft tops shoplifting," Chain Store Age, November 6, 2014.

Wojnarowicz, Krystyna, "Industrial Internet of Things in the maritime industry," Black Duck Software, February 11, 2015.

www.ingramcontent.com/pod-product-compliance
Lightning Source LLC
La Vergne TN
LVHW051229050326
832903LV00028B/2309

VUE
IN A NUTSHELL

A Practical Guide
To Master Vue

David Mark